Playing House

Author's Note

I have observed elsewhere that there is a significant difference between the truth of experience and the facts of everyday life. What I write about in these pages is often emotive, what I experienced, observed, and felt in different parts of my life. Some of the details I've forgotten (and occasionally I make note of that in the text), and some I've remembered, perhaps imperfectly. So I may not have all the facts in exact order, but I have no doubt about the truth of these stories.

Books by Lauren Slater

The $60,000 Dog: My Life with Animals

Blue Beyond Blue: Extraordinary Tales for Ordinary Dilemmas

Opening Skinner's Box: Great Psychological Experiments of the Twentieth Century

Love Works Like This: Moving from One Kind of Life to Another

Lying: A Metaphorical Memoir

Prozac Diary

Welcome to My Country

Edited by Lauren Slater

The Best American Essays 2006

The Complete Guide to Mental Health for Women

Beacon Press
www.beacon.org

Beacon Press books
are published under the auspices of
the Unitarian Universalist Association of Congregations.

16 15 14 13   8 7 6 5 4 3 2 1

This book is printed on acid-free paper that meets the uncoated paper ANSI/
NISO specifications for permanence as revised in 1992.

Text design by Ruth Maassen

Library of Congress Cataloging-in-Publication Data

Slater, Lauren.
  Playing house : notes of a reluctant mother / Lauren Slater.
    pages cm
  ISBN 978-0-8070-0173-8 (cloth : alk. paper) 1. Slater, Lauren—Family. 2.
Women authors, American—20th century—Biography. 3. Mothers—United
States—Biography. I. Title.
  PS3619.L373Z46 2013
  814'.6—dc23
  [B]
                                    2013013073

Parts of some chapters in this book were previously published in significantly dif-
ferent versions in the *New York Times*; *Self*; *Elle*; *Iowa Re-
view*; *Sun*; *Salon*; and in *Behind the Bedroom Door*, Paula Derrow, ed. (New York:
Delacorte Press, 2008); *Kiss Tomorrow Hello*, Kim Barnes and Claire Davis, eds.
(New York: Doubleday, 2006); *Searching for Mary Poppins*, Susan Davis and Gina
Hyams, eds. (New York: Hudson Street Press, 2006); *Coach*, Andrew Blauner, ed.
(New York: Grand Central Publishing, 2005); and *Maybe Baby*, Lori Leibovich,
ed. (New York: Harper Collins, 2006).

Playing House

Notes of a Reluctant Mother

Lauren Slater

BEACON PRESS

This one is for you, Benjamin.

Contents

Preface

I sometimes feel like flinching from the self portrayed in these pages, a self as selfish as she is honest. My hope is that the honesty redeems me, at least to some extent.

Without meaning to, thinking I was writing a series of separate pieces, I accidentally composed, over many years, a story of how I formed a family, the people I pulled around me, loving them so imperfectly, learning to love as we inched along, feeling for the contours of our space. Truthfully, I know very little about love. Just yesterday, driving my now-thirteen-year-old daughter to the orthodontist, she asked why she does not know her grandmother, my mother, who is a total absence in our lives. It was hard to explain to her then, as it is now in these pages (and I've tried), the wretched way we were under my parents' care, four children and a father perpetually pale, in flesh and spirit both. Eventually, when things got brutal enough, I left my family for a foster home and never went back, reuniting with my sisters and brother when I was well into my twenties and finding their faces as familiar as they were strange. How do you explain the severity of such a rupture to your daughter? How do you tell her that, in truth, you did not learn to love as a child and thus have come to the task of mothering with deep deficits? These pages describe the deficits and, equally as important, they describe my attempts to cope with them, to find my flame, my love, all crumpled and warped by water but still there and there for the taking. I took it and from it fashioned a house, a marriage, two fantastic children, and a train of enchanting animals to round out the shelter I built—birds, cats, dogs, and . . . a mule.

A mule? Why would anyone ever want a mule? In some sense this is what I am, sterile inside, an animal incapable of breeding or even of sex. Mules cannot perpetuate themselves, and thus, I must assume, they do not mate. These pages describe, in some metaphorical sense, a mule-woman, a woman who shuns sex, who could not believe she could care for children and therefore birthed two babies with deep misgivings. And yet, despite my obvious limitations, my brayings and buckings and truculence, I see in reading these pages that I have somehow learned to come around. I have shed the old matted fur of mental illness and frank violence and allowed myself to find enchantment in all the likely places, inside cupboards painted deep pink and the melted wells of scented candles that we, as a family, sometimes light on Chanukah, the flames flexible, bending, providing for me an alternate image, so the mule is replaced with warmth, from the outside and from the inside, too.

These pages mark the path I've walked—heeled, hooved, barefoot, clad and unclad, way up and deep down—to family, a constellation I've created even as it creates me, shaping me over and over again, I, changing with my children, who both tug and tether me, who lead me while I lead them, my husband here too. And so onward we go, we four, flickering, bickering, lost in a lacuna and found in much mud, with spoons and socks and pillows and pencils and all the other accoutrements of home; we hold on hard. We have each other. In the end—and there is, most definitely, an end—this is much, much more than enough.

Playing House

1

Tripp Lake

At the age of nine years I went to my first overnight camp, located in Poland, Maine, way up off 95, by a kidney-shaped lake where, across the shore, we could see the serrated lines of red roofs and, on sunny days, white sails walking along the water. The camp was called Tripp Lake, and it was for girls, or so my parents said, who were especially competitive, girls like me, not yet pubescent, packed with all the power of a life that has yet to really unfold, bringing with it the hard parts, the shames, the sadnesses, none of that yet. I wore my hair in what was called a "pixie cut," which was a nice way of saying it was short as a boy's, a crew cut really, and at that age white-blonde, so the stubble glittered silver in the summer sun. I spent my evenings playing capture the flag, an exhilarating game that requires fast feet and a bit of cunning.

Understandably, my parents thought it best to send me to a place where my energies could be shaped and expanded. I agreed. I thought I might be Olympic quality, like those skaters I'd seen or the skiers hunched over their poles, ricocheting down mountains where ice hung from all the trees.

I remember the first night at the camp, but no, let me begin before then, at the bus stop, about to leave and feeling, for the first time, a shudder of intense grief. My mother, an aloof woman whom I nonetheless adored, looked pale, her eyes foggy and distant. My father was a small man in the bakery business. Lately they'd been fighting. She wanted something grand out of life, something more than a muffin, whereas he was content to nozzle whipped cream on top of tarts. I loved my father, but I loved my mother more, more problematically is what I mean, in the crooked, hooked way only a daughter can.

I hugged my parents good-bye, and when I hugged my mother I could feel a circle of sadness in her. By leaving I felt as if I were betraying her. I had heard their voices at night, his quiet, hers shrill, *you* and *you* and *you*, and I'd seen my mother sometimes sitting on the porch looking out at nothing. She was a severe and brittle woman, and even at that age I knew brittle was breakable. Sometimes, driving in the car, she crushed the accelerator to the floor, just for the feeling of speed, and other times she cried with her mouth closed. I had the feeling, there at the bus stop, that she wished she were me, about to board a bus heading for the horizon, a green-striped bus with Peter Pan dancing on its flank and girls unabashedly eating apples. And because I felt her longing, inchoate, certainly unspoken, my chest seemed to split with sadness, and also guilt. This was a new emotion for me, an emotion that sat in the throat, an emotion that was maybe more imagistic than all the others. Guilt made me imagine that while I was away, my mother would come undone, her arm would fall off, her hair drift from her head. Guilt made me imagine that she would sit at night and cry, and what could I do about that? I wanted to say I was sorry, but I didn't really know what for. I couldn't have said it then, what I've since felt my whole life, that separation is a sword, painful, to be avoided at all costs.

My first night at camp: I could hear the flagpole rope banging against its post; I could hear the cry of what were maybe coyotes in the woods and the susurration of thousands of tree frogs. I couldn't sleep, so I stepped outside, onto the damp dirt that surrounded the cabin, and in the single spotlight that shone down I found a tiny toad, no bigger than a dime, with still tinier bumps on its taupe back. I lifted the amphibian up. I could not believe god or whoever could make an animal so small, an animal that would have, if I cut it open, all the same organs as me, in miniature, the locket-sized heart, bones like white wisps. How easy it is to break an animal; I could have crushed that frog with my fist, and part of me wanted to, while another part of me wanted to protect it, while still a third part of me wanted to let it go.

Before camp I'd been a more or less happy girl, but that first night I couldn't sleep, and by morning a wild sadness had settled in me. Where was I? Where was she? Someday I would die. Someone somewhere was sick. It was as if a curtain had been pulled back to reveal the true nature of the world, which was terror, through and through.

I became, for the first time in my life, truly afraid that summer, and the fears took forms that were not good, that did not augur well for my later life, although I didn't know it then. That first day, sitting on the green lawn, watching a girl do a cartwheel and another girl mount the parallel bars, I developed an irrational fear that is still hard to explain; I became hyper aware of my own body, the swoosh of my blood and the paddling of my heart and the *huh huh huh*s of my breath, and it seemed amazing and tenuous to me, that my body did all of this without any effort on my part. As soon as I became aware of this fact—almost as though I'd discovered my lower brain stem and how it's hitched to the spinal cord—as soon as I came to consciousness about this, I thought, "I can't breathe." And truly, it felt like I couldn't breathe. I thought, "I am thinking about my breathing, and if I think too hard about my breathing, which you're not supposed to think about, I will concentrate it right away," and I swallowed hard, and then I became aware of all the minute mechanisms that comprise a swallow, and so I suddenly felt I couldn't swallow anymore. It was like the lights were going out in my body, while meanwhile, in front of me, girls did cartwheels on the green lawn, completely unaware that I was dying.

After that, the fears came fast and furious. I was afraid to think about walking because then I would fall; breathing, because then I would suffocate. Swallowing was the worst one of all, to suddenly feel that you have no way of bringing the world down into your throat, of taking it in, no way. I then became afraid of the camp dining hall with its vicious swordfish mounted on one wall and its huge bear head with eyes like my mother's, dull, distant eyes, eyes at once wild and flat. I became afraid of pancakes, of toothbrushes, of cutlery, of water, the counselors urging me into the lake, where fronds fingered through the murk and scads of fish darted by, making a current cool against my legs.

That first week at camp, I fished a dime out of my uniform pocket (we wore only blue-and-white standard-issue uniforms) and called my mother. From far, far away I heard her voice. When had her sadness started? With my father, or before that, with her mother, who insisted that she, the oldest of three girls, do endless tasks and child care, so she was never able to shoot marbles, too busy shining the silver? My mother, I knew, had been a good girl, exceedingly good, and because of that, she hated my grandmother. She called her "Frances," and all holidays were barbed affairs, my mother sniping at her mother, making faces at the food, because she, if only given the chance, could have done better.

My mother did not go to college, despite the fact that she's bright. In my imagination, when I construct a history for her because she's so closed about her own, she wants to be a singer on a lit stage, or she wants to be a painter with her canvas at a quiet lakeside. She wants something larger than her own life, larger than her husband's life, larger than the house and kids, where what she does all day is clean. Much, much later on, when I was near grown, after she and my father divorced, my mother would develop a passion for Israel, its military might, and she became fiercely, ragefully Zionistic, and, totally bursting the caul of her confinement, she smuggled Bibles into the USSR. But this was later, after she found an outlet for her energies, and if only I'd known that was going to happen, that she was going to get into something good, if only I'd known, maybe my fears would have been fewer.

From far away my mother answered the phone, and I said, "I want to come home," and she said, "Don't be a quitter, Lauren." She wanted a larger life for me, a life where girls stand on stages, take charge of a team, swim the length of a lake and back in a Speedo suit. But as long as she didn't have these things, I felt much too guilty to take them for myself. None of this did I say.

At camp, we were divided into teams, and every activity, from drama to Newcomb (a kind of volleyball), was cast as a competition. I watched the older girls run with their lacrosse sticks, cradling them close to their sides, the ball in the gut-string pocket a soft blur. I watched as we, the younger girls, were taught to dribble and to shoot. Part of me wanted fiercely to win these games, while a still larger part of me could not even allow myself to participate, for somehow I would be betraying my mother if I did.

I was put on the Tigers team. Every morning after breakfast, standing at attention beneath that mounted swordfish, we would sing:

Shielded by orange and black
Tigers will attack
Catching every cue
Always coming through

It was a summer of color war. I remember, in particular, a game called bombardment, which we played in the gym on rainy days, Tigers versus Bears. In this game, each side is given a whole raft of rubber balls, and the purpose is simply to hurl them at each other as hard as you can, and whoever gets hit, is out. Before I'd left home, maybe I could have played this game, but certainly not now. Brown rubber balls came whizzing through the air, smacked against the lacquered floor of the gym, ricocheted off a face or a flank, and one by one each girl got hit and so would sit out on the sidelines. I was so scared of bombardment that whenever we played it, I hung way in the back of the court, where the other team's balls could not reach me. And then one day, because of this, I lasted throughout the whole game; everyone on my team had been hit except me, everyone on the other team had been hit except a senior girl named Nancy, a fourteen-year-old who had one leg shorter than the other. Because of this, she had custom-made shoes, her left heel stacked high enough to bring her up even, so she didn't tilt. Out of the corner of my eye I'd watched Nancy walk; even with her shoes she was strangely clumsy, gangly, always giggling nervously just at the rim of a group of girls, her desire to be taken in palpable.

And now Nancy and I were the last two left in the game. Everyone on the sidelines was screaming *Go go go!* Nancy's skin was as pale as milk, the strands of veins visible in her neck. Her gimp foot, supported by the huge rubber heel of her sneaker, seemed to wobble. *Go go go*, but I couldn't do it. I couldn't hurl that ball at her. It seemed existentially horrible that we were called to do this sort of thing in the world, to live in a way so someone had to lose. I stood there, locked in place, mesmerized by her skin and her foot, while Nancy lifted the ball high above her head and hurled it towards me with as much muster as she could muster, and I just stood there and let the ball hit me on the hip. Nancy won. That was the only outcome I could tolerate.

It didn't take long for the counselors to realize that something was wrong with me. I cried all the time. During free swim I retreated into the fringe of woods. The woods were next to a red barn where horses hung their heads over stall doors and there were golden squares of hay. Somehow, being near the horses calmed me. I liked their huge velvety lips, their thoughtful mastications. I liked the way they almost seemed to slurp up hay. I liked their rounded backsides, their plumed tails; I even liked their scat, flecked with grain and sweet smelling. Still, whenever I enter a barn and smell that smell, I do a Proustian plunge back to that first barn and the chestnut ponies.

Riding was a camp activity reserved for the older girls. I began to watch those girls cantering around the ring, the horses seeping dark sweat on their muscular chests. The riding coach's name was Lisa. She was a wisp of a woman in tan jodhpurs with suede patches at the knees. Once, when I was alone in the barn, I found her riding clothes hung up on a hook near the tack room. I tried on her green hunt jacket. It hung huge on me, but it felt cozy, and on its lapel there was a tiny brooch in the shape of a dragonfly.

"Would you like to try?" Lisa asked me one day.

"I'm only nine," I said.

"Well," she said, "I have a horse who's only nine too. Maybe you would make a good match."

"What's his name?" I asked.

"What's yours?" she said.

"Lauren," I said.

"Smokey Raindrops," she said. "But we call him Rain."

Rain. What a beautiful name. It was more a sound than a designation. "Yes," I said.

In fact, I didn't get to ride Rain that day. First, all the counselors, along with Auntie Ruth, the camp director, had to discuss it. Should I have lessons even though that was not a part of my camp curriculum? Would that make me happy? They thought it might.

Riding is a sport that, like any other, requires doing more than just the circumscribed activity. There is the ritualistic preparation, like the waxing of skis or the oiling of strings or, in my case, the grooming before the tack. A few days later, Lisa showed me how to use a currying comb, pick a hoof, leaning down and cupping the hairy fetlock, lifting the leg, the shine of the silver shoe with six nail heads in it. Time passed. Days passed. I found caring for the horses soothing, and I found when I was at the stable by these big snorting animals that I could forget about my own breath and just breathe.

All through the summer Lisa taught me how to ride, alone, no other girl there. She taught me how to post, how to do dressage, how to jump. I learned to hoist myself up, foot in one stirrup, other leg flung over the broad rank back. "When you post," she said, "watch the left leg. As it extends, you rise." The trot of a horse is like a metronome. It synchronizes you. It hypnotizes you. Left foot rise. Left foot rise. Your whole mind funnels down into this foot, the flash of hoof in the summer sun. And I'll never forget the day Lisa taught me to canter, how she said, "Trot out, give him a kick with your inside foot," and suddenly the horse's tight trot broke into the rocking run, around and around the ring we went, so fast it seemed, the world blurring by in a beautiful way.

Riding is largely a singular sport. Although there are shows and red ribbons, first places and sixth places, it can still be done, nevertheless, with no attention to that. You cannot really play lacrosse or soccer unless you are playing against someone, and this against-ness requires that you see yourself as separate, with all that that implies. But horseback riding you may do alone in the woods, or in a dusty riding rink, or even in your mind, which can canter too. Riding is not about separation. It is not about dominance. The only person you might hurt is you. You are, at long last, without guilt.

Riding. It is about becoming one with the animal that bears you along. It is about learning to give and take, give the horse his head, take the reins and bring him up. It is about tack, the glorious leather saddles, and the foam-stained bits, which fascinated me, how Lisa would roll them in sugar and slide them into the animal's mouth, its thick tongue clamped. It is, more than anything else, about relationship and balance, and as Lisa taught me how to do these things—walk, trot, canter—a sort of peace settled in me, a working-through my mother and me, a way of excelling at no one's cost.

And so the summer progressed. The only thing I could not do well was jump. Each time we approached the fence, the horse seemed to sense my primordial fear, fear of the fence and fear of everything it contained, and it would bunch to a scuttering halt or, more humiliating, the horse would stop and then, with me uselessly kicking and kicking, it would simply walk over the bar. I watched Lisa jump. She was amazing, fluid, holding onto the horse's mane as she entered the air, her face a mixture of terror and exhilaration, the balanced combination that means only one thing: mastery.

One month into the camp season was visiting day. My parents arrived, carrying leathery fruit rolls and a new canteen for me. They seemed as separate as ever, not even looking at each other.

My mother was appalled at the condition of my wardrobe. My clothes stank of sweat and fur. The soles of my boots were crusted with flaking manure. That was the summer, also, when I started to smell. "What's this?" she said, flicking through my steamer trunk. "Do you ever do your laundry?" She pulled out a white shirt with black spatters of mud on it and stains beneath the armpits, slight stains, their rims barely visible. "Lauren," she said.

"What?" I said.

She pursed her lips and shook her head. She held the shirt out, as though to study it. And once again, I saw that look of longing cross her face, but this time it was mixed with something else. I saw the briefest flicker of disgust.

A few minutes later, she went into our cabin bathroom, which we called The Greenie. She closed the door. I stalked up to it, pressed my ear against its wood. What did I do with my body? What did she do with hers? I heard the gush of water from the tap, the scrunch of something papery. The bathroom had a lock, on my side only. Quietly, and for a reason I still cannot quite explain, I turned the lever and the bolt slid quietly into its lock.

A few minutes later, when she tried to get out, she could not. She rattled the knob. We were alone in the cabin. I stood back and watched. "Lauren?" she said. "Lauren?" Her voice hurt me. It was curved into a question, and when I didn't answer, the question took on a kind of keening. "Lauren, are you there? Open the door." I stood absolutely still. I was mesmerized, horrified, by the vulnerability in her voice, how small she suddenly seemed and how I was growing in size, seemingly by the minute. For some reason I suddenly pictured her trapped in a tiny glass bottle. I held the bottle in my hands. I could let her out, or leave her.

I let her out.

"What are you doing?" she said. She stared at me.

I stared back at her. I could see her sweat now; it ran in a trickle down the side of her brow. I wanted to wipe it away.

They left in the evening, when colored clouds were streaming across the sky. I stood in the parking lot and watched their station wagon rattle over the dirt road, raising clouds of dust. The next few days, I backslid. My fears returned. There was the problem with my breathing, but accompanying this obsession was now the need to walk backwards while counting. I saw for sure that I was growing while she shrank. I saw for sure that I was growing *because* she shrank. I also saw something pointed in me, some real desire to win. Hearing that bolt sink into its socket, there had been glee and power.

I stopped riding then. I stopped going to the stables. I stayed in my bunk. I wrote letters and letters to my mother, the act somehow soothing my conscience. *Love, Lauren XXX. Kisses and hugs. I love you.*

At last, after four days had passed, Lisa, the riding instructor, came to my cabin to get me. "You disappeared," she said.

"I'm sick," I said.

"You know," she said, "I never much liked my mother."

I stared at her. How had she known?

"What will you do?" she asked.

"I don't know," I said.

"Are you going to sit on a cot for the rest of your life?"

"Maybe," I said.

"Just sit there and cry?" she said, and there was, suddenly, a slight sneer to her voice.

I looked away.

"I once knew a girl," she said, "who spent her whole life going from hospital to hospital because she loved being sick. She was too scared to face the world. Is that you?"

I have thought of her words often: a premonition, an augur, a warning, a simple perception.

I followed Lisa back to the barn. It was noontime. The sun was high and hot. She brought Rain into the middle of the ring, tightened up his saddle strap, and tapped on the deep seat. "All aboard," she said.

Sitting high on the horse, I could smell the leaves. I could smell my own sweat and all it contained, so many contradictions.

"We're going to jump today," she said and set the fence at four feet high. "Now, cross your stirrups and knot your reins. A rider has to depend on her inner balance only."

I cantered towards the jump, hands on my hips, legs grasping. But each time, at the crucial moment of departure, Rain would screech to a halt, and I'd topple into his mane.

"He senses your fear," Lisa said.

At last, after the third or fourth try, she went into the barn and came back out with a long black crop. Standing in the center of the ring, right next to the jump, she swizzled the crop into the air, making a snapping sound. The horse's ears flashed forward. "You have to get over it," she said. I centered myself in the saddle. I cantered twice around the rink and then turned in tight towards the bar. Lisa cracked the whip, a crack I still hear today whenever I feel my fears and I do, I often do, but I rose up, arms akimbo, in this leap merged with the mammal, its heart my heart, its hooves my feet, we sailed into the excellent air. I did it. I had found a way to move forward.

2

Going Solo

I bought my first house all on my own, without a man or a friend or even much money to speak of. I bought it on a salary of $25,000 a year, in 1993, in a rundown section of Boston, where there were murderers and car thieves and kids smoking pot on porch stoops in the smog-filled summers. Everyone told me not to do it. The house was wrapped in vinyl siding with a gorgeous old slate roof and radon in the basement, and had peeling lead paint and windows so drafty the weather came through. My first winter in my brandnew house, I would wake up and find my counters and computer covered in small snow drifts, and my breath was visible, sterling silver Os in the air, if I pursed my lips just right, each O rising up towards the buckled ceiling like a little exclamation of pleasure or surprise. I wrapped myself in an afghan, bought a crock-pot, and made myself some stew.

I have always, always wanted to own my own home. This may have something to do with the fact that I had left my family for a foster home, and what I got in place of my own abode was a foster family I knew would never really be mine. I became aware, at a very young age, of DNA's sweeping spirals and how those spirals were like ropes binding you to your people, whom you could never replace. My foster family was good and kind, but in the nights I dreamt of houses, of finding a house in a cove or on a dark, deadend street and going inside and there seeing butter-yellow walls and stacks of colorful quilts and white rabbits on tiled tables and rooms. The dreams always featured me, lone and lost, entering what looked like a normal or even suspicious-looking house to find that it unfolded endlessly, room upon room, garden upon garden, terraces unseen from the street, a horse with his head hanging in the kitchen window, a bowl of bright cherries in every cupboard.

I eventually left my foster family and went to college and lived in a dorm my first year, which I despised, with its cinderblock walls and stained couches and cold, iron beds. Then I rented a house off-campus with three friends, which I liked somewhat better, but the house wasn't mine. I wanted, more than a man, a best friend, a child, or talent, I wanted to own my own home because I knew that as soon as it became mine, it would become magical, the "mine" and "magical" conflated here, ownership as fairytale.

I was thirty and working as a literacy instructor when I decided it was time to buy. I'd just gotten my first book deal and it had left me with some extra cash. I wanted a huge house with at least seven rooms so I could paint each in one of the seven spectrum colors and thus have a rainbow on my hands. I found a two-thousand-square-foot dump, my neighbor on one side an old lady with orange hair, and on the other side a convicted murderer with a bracelet on his ankle. In the nights, police-car lights swished by on my walls. The crime rate was high. My father, whom I'd reconnected with, told me not to do it, a waste of money, and what did I, a single woman, need with so much space? My boyfriend of the time was miffed. I knew I wouldn't marry him, and even if he were "the one," why should I wait, and who, really, could accompany me in the pursuit of this deeply private dream? I didn't buy a house in which to start a marriage or a family; I bought a house to right old wrongs, to fix my past—not to form my future; I bought a house so I could, once and for all, prove to myself that the roof over my head was of my own making, and if wind or weather or sheer bad luck tore it away, I'd find it again. I could afford it, in every sense of that word.

I moved into my new house in early summer. Within ten minutes of getting the keys, I had torn off the drop ceilings to find the old pressed tin beneath. Within three days I had the floors painted. I didn't want wood; I wanted white, and turquoise, sea and sand,

and blue, so it would be like walking on a hard enamel sky. In the attic closet I found three old, curved canes with the word *Noam* carved into the wood: Noam, like gnome.

My enthusiasm for rehabilitation that summer knew no bounds. I started work on the exterior of the house by tearing off the tilted, rotting porch and ripping up the floorboards and replacing them with fir. I was a one hundred percent u-do-it gal, working on my own with little plan or skill. Call it confidence, or ecstasy, or beginner's luck: all my projects went well. Nails sunk swiftly into wood. Paint painted itself onto freshly spackled walls. Then something happened.

I was working on the porch in the hot summer sun. I was digging four-foot holes in which I planned to place new posts to hold up the new floor. I swung my pick and from deep in the earth I heard the sound of something moan and clang. I stopped. The moan was like a person, buried alive, while the clang had the mournful echo of a hollow pipe. I swung again. Again this echoing moan, and then a geyser of water sprang up from the ground, a fountain with all the force of someone's rage; I had hit a waterline. Water spread across the ground, under the powdery foundation of my home, and, when I ran inside, I saw it seep up between the kitchen floorboards. It just kept coming. I was in it up to my ankles, this wellspring, this never-ending *source* of what I was not sure. And in an instant all my ecstasy and confidence was replaced with total bone-freezing fear: I couldn't do it, I was fundamentally alone, I would drown, or get electrocuted, or simply float forever in some unclaimed and unnamed space. By the time the plumbers came I was crying. By the time the leak, to put it mildly, was fixed, the ground outside my home had eroded and my first floor smelled like wet dog.

Soon after that, men came with what they called a French drain and suctioned the water out of my house, but it took days and days to dry, and the wood warped. I calmed down. What was wrong with a little warp and wobble here and there? I had dreamt of houses, old suspicious-looking houses with many wonders in them; this could be one. A long time ago, I recalled, when I left my first home, never to return, I had taken with me a tiny floor tile, pried it loose, held it close in my palm as the car drove me away forever. I had the floor tile with me then, and I still do now. Two nights after the furious fountain burst, I found the tile in a box left unpacked. It was blue-and-white striped. I held it up to the light and it gleamed like an old eye. I redid the ruined floor with tile this time. I found beautiful green-floral tiles in a steep sale, and I laid square by square. I laid it all down. With the flat of my putty knife, I creamed in the white grout. In the center of my brand-new floor I placed the small blue piece from my past, where for years it had stared at me, it now affirmed me, saying (and still saying), "You last."

3

Paired

When I first met my husband, I thought his beard was sexy. It was a shadow of stubble, the color of iron filings, giving him a look that was at once tattered and tough. The fact that my husband is neither of these things—he is a chemist and a self-proclaimed Druid—only added to the appeal. I loved my husband's beard, the way it hovered halfway, how it felt against my skin, both soft and sharp. I came to know his face by the presence and particularities of this beard. I was attracted to him in part because of this beard. It would not be entirely wrong to say I married my husband based on his beard; based on other things too, of course—his humor, his intelligence, his kindness, his quirkiness—but the beard was a factor.

Before we married—while we were courting, that is—my husband took care of his beard. When it started to get fluffy, he trimmed it with a tiny pair of sewing scissors and a black electric razor. But after we married—I don't know exactly when, a year, maybe two—once we were settled down into domesticity, once our relationship had lost the anxious edge that comes without commitment, he started to let his beard go. He started to let it grow. It came in curls and frizz, and it seemed to spread sideways more than down, making his face look fat. Once during this time he took a business trip, and when I came to pick him up at the airport I was shocked to see him with the clarity that comes from absence. He looked like an old-fashioned lumberjack, or Moses, his lips barely visible, fully fringed with hair. He also appeared crazed. He got into the car, tossing his suitcase in the back.

"How are you?" he said, and he leaned over to kiss me. The beard had a strange smell, a smell familiar but impossible to place, the inside of an old trunk maybe, cedar chips and dust. I flinched and drew away. "What's wrong?" he said.

"Nothing," I said, and I hated myself then, hated myself for the lie and also for my superficiality.

We were mostly quiet on the way home. The highway hummed under our wheels, the long ribbon of road unfurling before us, green signs flashing in the headlights and then yanked back into blackness. As we pulled into our driveway, I said, "You know, I think you should cut your beard."

He pulled on it and smiled. "I kinda like it this way," he said.

"I don't think I do. You remind me . . . I mean, you don't look like my husband. You look . . . avuncular. I really think you should trim it at least."

"It's my beard," he said.

"But I'm the one who kisses it," I said. "I wouldn't be surprised if a bat flew out of that mess."

"Cool," he said. "A bat in my beard. I like it."

My husband then swung open the car door, bounded up our front steps. The dogs were ecstatic when they saw him. They leapt up, barked, and he funneled his face down close to theirs, tongues slurping, wet noses, and when he looked up, his beard had some slobber on it.

I was grumpy then. Days passed and the grumpiness would not leave. And then, one week later, my husband came home and his beard was gone. Presto. Poof. I had never, ever seen the lower half of his face in plain light before. There it was, stark, white, white, stark, pale, plucked; he looked young, very young, the shaved skin red as a diaper rash. I hate to say it but I yelped. It was as though he had snuck up on me wearing a Halloween mask, only the mask was his actual face, and his actual face was as unfamiliar as a stranger's.

"You like?" he said.

"Why'd you do that?" I said.

"You asked me to," he said.

"I said trim your beard, not strip it."

"I want to try out a beardless identity. I want to pass as a Republican."

"What," I said, irritated, "you think a beard is radical? I'm sure the Christian Right has a large bearded base."

"You know," he said, "you look a little scared."

"You should have warned me," I said. "You don't look anything like yourself."

"It's me," he said, and of course he was right. It was him, and that was precisely the problem.

Everyone likes to think that looks are secondary in love. We pick our partners for their talents, their brilliance, their ambition, their stature. Sure, we like a handsome man, but we don't walk the aisle based on a face; we are holistic; we understand beauty is emitted in many ways, and comes in many shapes and sizes. This is what we like to tell ourselves. But in fact, recent studies have shown that human beings tend to favor (i.e., love) the people in their lives who are most attractive. In a 2005 study, researchers at the University of Alberta gathered some disturbing results after hanging out in supermarkets and watching mothers interact with their children. They found that mothers gave more praise and positive reinforcement to their more beautiful children. Other studies have shown that people with conventionally pretty faces are more likely to be picked for job offerings and are more likely to advance up the corporate ladder. In his study on mate selection, psychologist David Buss showed a series of faces to people from Katmandu to Kentucky, and whatever the culture, everyone seemed to agree on which faces were the most attractive. As human beings, we know beauty, and we love beauty. I did not find my beardless husband beautiful. He had no chin.

What happens when the partner we pick gets too fat, or too thin, or too . . . chinless or . . . something? I felt I was falling out of love, or out of attraction. I did not want to have sex with this man. That night we did have sex and it was creepy, the foreign face floating above mine, the moon peeping in our window. I wanted, more than anything, to feel the click of connection, but it wasn't there. I kept saying to myself, "This is Benjamin, Benjamin, Benjamin," but it seemed he'd shaved more than his beard; he'd shaved his self. Without his beard, his voice sounded different to me, higher and more hollow, as though he were not quite real, as though a motor ticked inside him. It was a subtle shift. His voice sounded different to me the same way a piano sounds different when it's slightly out of tune. You keep pressing the note you know, and it keeps coming back at you all the more warped because it has within it the sound of something familiar, but far away. Later that night, when Benjamin was asleep, I got up and pulled out our wedding album. Now there was the man I'd married.

Understand, I wanted to learn to love beardless Benjamin. In fact, I wanted to learn to love and be desirous of my husband in whatever guise he came in. To that end I decided what I needed to do was desensitize myself to his new face, force it into neutrality, whereupon, perhaps, I could learn to love it. I had a whole desperate theory worked out. It went like this: He had shocked me by shaving his beard and not telling me. I now associated his shaven face with shock, discomfort, even fear, and because of these associated emotions, I was bound to think he was ugly. Therefore, I needed to look at him beardless as much as possible. I needed to stare at his face, feel his face, run my fingers over his chinny chin chinlessness, come to recognize the blades of bones that had been hidden beneath his hair. I did this. Over dinner, in bed, I would lay the flat of my hand against him; I would touch him like a blind person, searching for clues, for the familiar . . . *oh, it's you!* I went so far as to study his new face beneath a magnifying glass, when he was sleeping, of course, his pores huge, stalks of stubble struggling up through the pocked skin. Oh dear. He woke up. "What are you doing?" he said.

"Studying you," I said.

"You hate the way I look without a beard," he said. "I know."

I didn't say anything.

"I'm not going to grow it back," he said. "Not right now."

"I don't think I can adjust," I said. "If I got really, really fat, like, two hundred pounds, I think you would have the right to tell me you weren't comfortable with that." Even as I said this, I was not sure it was so true.

"Maybe I would have that right," he said. "But I wouldn't exercise it. Besides, I like a little real estate on a woman."

I asked my friend C. about it. Her husband, V., was a carpenter, trim, muscular, dark. Then he took time off to be home with his kids and before long his stomach was lapping over his belt, and a few months after that, plain and simple, he was obese. "Are you still attracted to him?" I asked.

"No, not really," she said.

"Does that bother you?" I asked.

C. paused. We were sitting in her kitchen, sipping coffee. "You know," she said, "we have two kids. I work full time. I'm tired at the end of the day. He's tired too, more so because now he's out of shape. We've stopped having sex. I get a lot more sleep. And if I had to choose between sex and sleep, I'd pick sleep."

I asked my friend D. She had once had a boyfriend who got nose cancer, and they had to take off his nose. He was lucky, in that that stopped the cancer, but now he was maimed and had to wear a prosthetic nose held on by a band.

"What did you do?" I said.

"We broke up," she said.

"Because he had no nose?"

"I wouldn't put it that way," she said. "The cancer illuminated a lot of things for us, ways in which we were not compatible."

"So it had nothing to do with the nose," I said.

"That's what I like to tell myself," she said, and then she touched her own nose, as though it might be growing.

I'm quite sure that I could not love a beautiful dummy, a stocky blond jock who watched football while tossing peanuts in his mouth. However, during the beardless crisis, I learned that I could not feel eros towards a man I found odd looking. And the old saying "To know him is to love him" just holds no water for me. Obviously, I knew my husband when he shaved off his beard or let it grow too long, and, sad to say, whatever inner beauty he had was temporarily blocked by his surface sheen, at least when it came to sex. Lunch, dinner, chess, hanging out, talking, none of that was affected, but sex is about bodies, it is about skin, surface touching surface; sex is superficial, and, as it turns out, the superficial is pretty profound.

After my husband went baby-faced, I started doing some research into evolutionary psychology, specifically as it relates to sex. I spoke with anthropologists Helen Fisher and Elaine Hatfield, each of whom told me that beauty—our perception of it, that is—plays a crucial role in the survival of our species. According to these experts, we love/are attracted to beautiful people, those with symmetrical faces, proportioned bodies, and so on because these people are frequently the healthiest, and although we do not know it, we select our mates based on their ability to perpetuate our little packet of genes.

This explanation comforted me. It did not bring the beard back to my husband's face, but it did let me off the hook, at least a little bit. All right, so I was not a corrupt product of advertising culture, at least not totally. I was responding to an ancient limbic drive, protecting the babies that would one day be mine, yearning for symmetry, a chin, sanguinity to pass on down the line. "Beards," Helen Fisher told me, "signify a man with a lot of testosterone, and that's why women find them attractive."

One would think, then, that the bigger the beard, the hotter the guy. But somehow it doesn't work that way.

"Did you know, honey," I said to my husband over dinner that night, "a beard signifies a good supply of testosterone?"

"Really?" he said. He smiled at me. "So if you shave your beard does your testosterone level drop?"

"I don't know why you wouldn't grow the beard back for me," I said.

"Maybe if you stopped asking I would," he snapped.

So I stopped. Weeks passed. I ceased being shocked, but in shock's place was a sort of dullness, a certain reserve.

Then a friend of Benjamin's from college came to visit. "Hey, Benjamin," he shouted as he came in. "You finally shaved off that beard. God, you look so much better without it."

"You think so?" I said.

"If there is one thing I've learned over years of shaving and growing facial hair," said Benjamin, "it's that people always, always prefer you how they met you originally. No one who met me without a beard has ever really liked my beard, and no one who met me with a beard has ever really thought I look good without one."

"I met you with a beard," I said.

"That's obvious," he said.

What exactly is the beauty we pursue to protect our progeny? Some studies have shown that people find symmetrical faces the most beautiful, but I wonder if beauty is best defined by familiarity. It's not that there is some objective standard out there; we love what we know, and what we call lovely is really solace, home. In the 1950s, one of psychology's greatest scientists, Harry Harlow, did a series of fascinating experiments with baby monkeys. These experiments were, in their own way, horrible, but like a horror movie, they revealed something essential about what it means to love and to be loved. Harlow removed baby rhesus monkeys from their mothers and raised them in isolated cages with mannequin mothers who were wired up to deliver milk. Some of these mannequin monkey mothers were not quite finished by the time the batch of babies were born, so some babies had mannequin mothers with just a plain wooden ball for a head—no face, no monkey mouth, no simian eyes, no features, nothing. And because this was the only mother these monkeys had, they each came to love their faceless mannequin, and to cling to her, and to drink from her wired milk supply. A few weeks later, Harlow and colleagues painted faces on their incomplete monkey mannequins. They painted beautiful simian faces with eyes of gentleness and color. But when the baby monkeys saw these faces, they screamed, and with their little hands, reached out and turned the wooden ball of the head so the face faced backwards, and they were again in the embrace of the flat, featureless nothingness that for them was home, was whom they loved.

The first face may always be the most beautiful face. When we find a partner attractive to us perhaps we are not really thinking *take me with you* so much as *bring me back.* Six years later my husband was bearded again, and I noticed his strawberry-blond beard was going gray, flecked here and there, and his eyes seemed tired. One night, he pointed out to me his bald spot, a circle widening slowly on the crown of his head, the exposed scalp pink as a salmon, too vulnerable looking to touch. "Will you love me when I'm old and bald?" he said.

"Yes," I said. I somehow knew I would. Which, of course, contradicts everything I have just said. I know how an evolutionary psychologist would explain this contradiction: no longer in reproductive mode, I will no longer need his beauty. And he will no longer need any of mine. In other words, I will love him without eros. Of course this explanation falls prey to the assumption that the elderly do not need beauty because they do not have sex. I can't comment on this right now, although I'm sure I will when my time comes, if I should be so lucky. When I am old and toothless, when he is gray and wrinkled . . . I think, if I get there, I will just be happy to have him near me—I will think, *This is Benjamin*—someone to sleep with in the truest, most literal sense, side by side as our days begin to darken.

4

On Fire

My husband caught on fire smack-dab in the middle of our marriage, right around that inevitable but destabilizing romantic dip when all that had once waxed now suddenly waned, even the actual moon seeming to be—night in, night out, never changing—just a sliver of stone, or maybe my spouse's fingernail cutting found on the back of our bathroom floor, signaling for sure a careless man whose spontaneity had somehow turned to sloppiness. His droppings, it seemed, were everywhere.

At night during this time, I would lie awake and listen to the sound of my mate snoring, alarms going off in my body. What would bring us back? Little did I know that in just a matter of months those inner alarms would turn outer, the whole house going off as white smoke, almost creamy in its consistency, filled the rooms and the detectors shrieked, a sound so particular, so piercing, it caused our dog to go deaf in one ear even as it signaled, for us, the return of our senses—sound as well as sight, smell, taste, and, for a wonderful while, touch.

But I'm ahead of myself here, because the fire came in mid-May, a beautiful, balmy month, while for the time being I was still stuck in the sliver-stone of my moon and marriage in the New England winter when the snow was starch white as it fell but turned tattered, gritty, almost the instant it touched down on the urban ground, strewn with broken glass, dented tin cans, candy wrappers crackling in the wind.

It was a cold, cold time, that winter. Snow piled higher than our porch windows, and when the melt finally came, it oozed through the pores of the screens and rotted the painted porch floor. We'd been together, my husband and I, the proverbial seven years, each year before the seventh year, an A- or B+, in no particular order, seesawing grades we could do more than accept; grades we could celebrate, for we were mature and understood no union is as perfect as it once was, as it was the day, the moment, the second you first fell in love.

We hadn't had children yet. We hunted for mushrooms around the banks of the city's polluted pond, parting the rotting grasses to find the enormous ears of fungi that Benjamin, my husband, a scientist, identified for me. We ordered every book Frank L. Baum, author of the *Wizard of Oz*, had ever written and read the volumes out loud before bed, ferreted into magical worlds where fruit trees grew tiny plum-colored people, their umbilical cords the stem attaching head to tree, until the sun finally finished its ripening and the miniature people dropped to the ground and began their bipedal lives. My husband and I had sex and fruit and fairytales, and for dinner we grilled steak-sized portobellos sautéed in thick pats of butter, the smell everywhere.

And then that seventh winter came, carrying with it cloud sacks stuffed with snow and some mean man who lived right over the horizon weaving a wind whose edges he honed on a grinding stone as sharp as a shark's smile. By January most everyone in Boston looked faintly anemic and wind-bitten; by February there was widespread talk of light therapy. Storm followed storm followed storm, and while I wouldn't blame the demise of my marriage entirely on the weather, I would not hesitate to say it helped us down in a hefty way. Traits that had once seemed charming were now serious irritants. My husband's skin, which had been a beautiful Scandinavian fair, had somehow, somewhere, in some way, turned faintly pinkish, and sometimes this phrase leapt into my mind: "*I have married a pink man.*" For his part, he became critical of my thickening waistline and my less-than-perfect flossing habits. We began to bicker, and then we began to be bitter.

In general, people refer to this phase in monogamy as the "seven-year itch," a term I dislike, implying, as it does, that a tube of cortisone cream or, in a very bad case, perhaps a titrating dose of prednisone would do the trick. But anyone who has ever been through this, this marital or relational *itch*, can tell you the phenomenon to which we are here referring cannot be solved with a scratch. And why not? Because it is not an itch to begin with. Itch is an itchy word, its *ch-ch* sound suggests some perseverative, compulsive yearning, some . . . some . . . *urge* for an *answer* that would, in this case, come not with words but with someone scratching . . . skin. Your skin. His skin. My skin. In my own case, I didn't want my husband touching my skin, because he had begun to bother me in too many minor mundane ways. This was in no way an itch. It lacked any quality of intense neural focus. What we had was more like a lesion, essential cords cut, and the result: numbness.

Researchers have found that in healthy pair-bonded relationships, there are in general five positive interactions for every negative one. Switch it around and you can catch the powerful punch of this measurement tool more easily. It's called "the five to one rule." In bad relationships, in fact in reliably *doomed* relationships, there are always two or more insults for every six interactions the couples have. It's good I didn't know this at the time or I might have thrown in the towel, perhaps even all our towels, so that, when the fire was eating my husband's body alive, he would not have had anything to beat back the flames with.

As it turns out, I hadn't tossed in the towel the night my husband combusted, but neither did I have one handy, and even if I had, shock would probably have prevented me from offering it to him as I stood there, on the threshold of his study, and watched and heard (how horrible to hear; the hearing is what still, to this day, ignites my mind with terror) his raw human screams as the crazy flames, propelled by a chemical he'd spilled, made a crackling orange halo out of what had once been his beautiful hair.

We sought couple's counseling, but now, years later, I recall few of the specifics. There was a square office done in pleasing neutrals, abstract art on the walls. What I most recall was the counselor's foot. It always had on it a very high heel that dangled halfway off, so her heel was in the raw, except for the nylons that netted it. She used all the standard phrases—*baggage, communication, childhood, repetition compulsion.* In her own way, I suppose, she was healing, as our joint dislike of both her and the process gave Benjamin and me something to bitch about together.

Given the givens, the fact that the rough ride of my marriage was not at all unusual, that many, if not most couples, could tell a story with the same general spine, even if the specifics of the structure were different—one would think that marriage counseling would have evolved into a state at least as high tech as your average PC. The numbers themselves suggest a national emergency. If, according to the latest census, about half of all American couples have children, and of those more than half divorce, then, well, *why get married at all?* It's not a question asked with tongue in cheek. Everywhere one looks, in the animal world, that is, are ample examples of why marriage, the product of culture, is doomed in the nest of nature, where culture has no choice but to reside. Even the much-touted prairie vole, feted for its fierce lifelong monogamy, has recently been discovered to have illicit affairs, like so many other animal species probably in search of the dopamine high that comes with a fresh mate newly bedded.

It has been definitively established that monogamy, while good for safe sex, babies, and probably income, is not really the way of the naked natural world. Take, for instance, the phenomenon researchers call "the Coolidge effect." Discovered in the 1950s, the Coolidge effect has had ample time to demonstrate its impressive reliability and validity, which is that when you drop a male rat into a cage with a receptive female rat, you see an initial frenzy of copulation. Then, progressively, the male tires of that particular female. Even without an apparent change in her receptivity, the male rat reaches a point where he has little libido left, and, eventually, he simply ignores the female. However, if you replace the original female with a new one, the male immediately revives and begins copulating again. You can repeat this process with fresh females until the rat nearly dies of exhaustion.

The rat's renewed vigor does not reflect an increase in his well-being—although it will look (and perhaps temporarily feel to him) that way. The rat's vigor comes from surges of a neurochemical called dopamine, which floods the reward circuitry of his primitive brain so that he gets the job done.

That seven-years-ago seven-year itch. The first bland stretch in my marriage. The itch that was not an itch, or even an ache; just numbness. Staring at my husband and seeing him as stone, or salt, the flattening out severe. Words dwindled down between us, and when I touched him, his skin felt less like flesh than wax.

We made it through that winter of winds and endless snow. Eventually spring came, an anemic tentative thing, the first crocuses a yellow so pale they seemed somehow vitamin deficient, but over time, the warm air found its way through. And then came a balmy night in late May, the sort of night when the windows are open and fresh air pours in by the jugful, and you would be happy if you weren't so sad, because June, the month of roses, is right around the corner. I was in the kitchen washing a pot, moving the sponge round and round the pot's curved contours, watching the bubbles froth up and wash away with the water running over my hands, mesmerized by the sight of these bubbles bubbling and then dissolving, over and over again, until, all of a sudden, in a second that changed my life forever, I heard a scream the likes of which I had never, ever heard before.

This was before we had children, so I knew the scream, clearly coming from the basement of the house, where my husband had his study, belonged to him. The scream was strangled in its sound but also blood curdling and continuous, the scream of a man in the grip of total terror, the scream making the man at once larger than life while stripping him to his primitive once-was essence, the scream for the mother even as it was the mother of all screams. I put down the pot and took the steps down to the cellar three at a time, but even so, I was going so slowly I could not get to the bottom fast enough, there were so many steps, not ten, like I'd thought, there were suddenly thousands upon thousands of steps unfolding accordion-like in front of me. The scream continued, as did the steps, on and on, for seconds, moments, months, years, yes, *years* went by before I finally hit the concrete ground and began making my way across the ocean of floor, towards the scream, towards the story behind the scream, another endless trip, crossing that expanse of dusty floor, like traveling to China on the slowest of slow boats, as the blood-curdling screams (for they were plural now, not a single desperate sound but a series of separate sounds, each one more terrible than the next) continued on for all those years and universes.

And then I reached my husband's study door and flung it open. I had already decided in my mind what I would find, and this fixed decision only increased my shock at finding something so different than my vision. Prior to opening the study door, I'd assumed my husband was being murdered, for what else could cause such sounds of total terror? I'd assumed a murderer had snuck in through the basement window and was slowly, very slowly, slitting my husband's throat so he died in terrible torture. I expected to find the murderer there and the wet red of blood, but as is often the case, my mind did not meet the moment at any point. I saw my husband standing there, screaming, a smashed test tube on the floor. The smoke was as creamy as it was noxious, but who cared? His entire body was on fire. Have you ever seen a person burn? A log burns from its inner heart, but a person burns from his outer edges. My husband was rimmed by flames dancing down his periphery, outlining him in leaping light, from head to toe, except his hair, which was engulfed, like he was wearing a top hat of swarming fire, a semitransparent Cat-in-the-Hat hat that showed his singular strands of hair as they were being incinerated. He had long hair at that time, long, fine, beautiful strawberry-blond locks that usually fell straight as rain to his shoulders but that were now all standing up like porcupine quills, offering themselves erect to the moving mouth of the fire.

What happened next is unclear. My husband says I tried to run away, but I know this is untrue. I know for sure there was this nanosecond moment of extreme existential distress when I was thinking a thought as long and complex as the Torah but that I could start and finish in a sliver of a second, and the thought went something like this: *Less than a moment ago I was a woman washing a pot, but now I am a woman watching her lover burn to death in a fire, and forever after this I will always be a woman who watched her lover burn to death in a fire. Of all the possible life narratives I could have, this, it turns out, will be mine, forever and ever, because the present, even as I am thinking this, is cementing into the past, and how odd, I never expected such a story to be mine, that I am a woman who once watched her husband burn to death in a fire, but it just goes to show, you never know what story, in the end, you'll be stuck with.*

And then I recall dashing into the room, which was by now aflame in several spots, only one of those spots was the body of my husband. I remember grabbing him and trying to pull him out of his study, for there were very flammable chemicals stashed everywhere in this room and soon—at any moment—the whole house would surely explode into a fireball high in the warm night air; we would glow in our incineration, so *come now! Run now!* I recall trying to pull him out as he, with his bare hands, plunged them into the thicket of fire on his head and the fringes of fire on his body, squelching the flames with his bare hands, slamming his hands onto his body again and again, starving that fire of air, smashing the O out of it, and then, successful, racing back *into* the burning room and grabbing the fire extinguisher with his crisped hands, saying, "*Shit shit shit,*" as he fumbled for the plug you never think you'll have to pull. He pulled it, and the extinguisher ejaculated hissing white foam that instantly quelled the impish, vicious, spreading fire, his entire study dusted down with a frozen smoking white. "Run now!" I screamed, and we ran; all the smoke detectors dancing and swiveling on the ceilings, shrieking their singular song over and over again, unable to calm down until I'd thrown open every window and we had watched the white ghosts of smoke take off into the night air, Caspers, each one, they lifted off and drifted up, up, at last out of reach, dispersing into particles of our past. My husband was alive.

I remember running to the freezer, then, and throwing all its contents at him: the frozen peas, pints of Ben and Jerry's, bagels in a bag, cubes of ice squared in their plastic trays, throwing everything frozen straight at him while saying, over and over and over again, "I love you I love you I love you," standing on tiptoes to kiss his crumbling lips, my own lips, later, dark with char, "I love you," and then hurling at him as hard as I could a bag of frozen string beans—wack wack wack—he was so stunned, everything fell at his feet. At last, when the freezer was emptied, I picked up the packages and pressed the crystallized bags to his curling skin, already starting to ooze.

I love you.

The fact is, our seven-year itch ended then, ended high on the flames of his near death, ended in the stench of smoke and the run-down batteries of all our alarms. We both had enough adrenaline emptied into our bodies to last us another seven years, which is probably just what happened, because now it is seven years later and, well, perhaps I should torch him tonight?

Coda

It's winter again; it's dark in here again; no, don't give me a match. I don't want a conflagration just so I can know I love him, but what about, tonight, a controlled campfire, after the children are asleep, in the cold November air? I can picture it, the forked flames, the delicious smell of lit logs, our voices, when we speak, very visible. I see silver smoke—a sign of safety—and also a time for us to talk. If I can see it, then does this mean we might do it? We'd have to bundle up and find the wood. We'd have to strike a match and touch its tip to what was once a tree. Who knows, maybe we'd even lie back on the frosted grass and watch the smoke spin up. On and on, up and up, the sky would turn us tiny, together, two imperfect people so imperfectly paired, these facts ashes in the face—in the space—of vastness. The fire would crackle; the heat would seep; we'd press together and tilt our faces skyward, smoke rising, this couple called *us* watching their ghosts go.

5

Uncurling

Every house has its finest piece of furniture: the heirloom bed your Aunt Bonnie gave you, the Chippendale table; in mine, it's my medicine cabinet. My medicine cabinet is huge, handsome, with painted angels and delicate scrollwork rimming a mirror of finest glass. Open it up. Inside this antique are bottles filled with all manner of modern pills—Prozac in sleek, bicolored bullets; shining orange Klonopins; little lithiums in a dazzle of white. I take these pills every day, to keep my mind intact.

I have mental illness. That's an unfortunate phrase, *mental illness*, as old fashioned as the cabinet that houses my cures. I wish for a different descriptor, something both mythic and modern, like *chemical craziness*, like *brain bruise*. My particular form of illness is called obsessive-compulsive disorder, with a dash of depression thrown in. Years have gone by when my whole head was hot, when hospitals have been a haven. I had my first hospitalization when I was fourteen, because I could not stop cutting myself. I no longer cut. Now I count, in increments of three. I count to keep planes from falling out of the sky, to keep the moon in orbit. I count for luck and safety.

My red-headed husband and I did what married people do: we got pregnant. I will never forget the test I took. Six in the morning, standing in the half-dark bathroom, watching a blue cross swim up on the white test wand, *yes*. The cross was a warning and a wish. I closed my eyes and said, "Go."

I did not want to have a child. Before she came to me, and before I came to love her, I dreaded the thought of motherhood, all those hours spent on the playground or in Chuck E. Cheese's. I had heard women talk about "baby lust" and knew I possessed not a drip, not a drop, the drive towards procreation almost absolutely absent in me. My husband wanted our first. Motherhood went against my nature, which is brooding and acerbic and self-consumed. Plus there was my wayward mind, an issue. "And what about your illness?" friends said to me. "How will you mother when you struggle so much with anxieties and depression?" These are good questions. I'd spent my adolescence and young adulthood in mental hospitals, and then one day I swore I'd never go back. And I did not. I have not. I found my place and people. But still, the symptoms come, no matter what my will or situation. So here's my question: Should a woman who is mentally ill become a mother? Are mental illness and motherhood by nature mutually exclusive? Was this a mistake, and a selfish one to boot?

My doctor, the one who has treated me for more than a decade, was definitive. "It is dangerous for you to have a baby," he pronounced. "You have too many periods of instability." Still, something in me said *go*.

Months went by. My belly bulged. Sometimes people asked me whether I was worried I might pass my bad genes on to my child. I didn't mind that question even though, when I think about it now, it seems crude and unkind, assuming, as it does, that genes are both omnipotent and simplistic. My genes are difficult genes, different genes, but I'm not sure they're *bad*. After all, the same genetic structure that drives me to check and tap also spurs me to put words on a white page, to garden until the yard is a riot of reds, yellows, and delphinium blues each summer. My genes, like everyone else's I think, are both flower and thorn, little twisted things on their cones of chromosomes, such surprising, complex shapes.

These shapes, however, can be difficult to hold. Illness, without doubt, is a challenge. There has been a lot of talk about the contemporary female dilemma of juggling two balls, motherhood plus career. But there is a third ball here, and it has been overlooked: mental illness. According to the National Institute of Mental Health, one out of eight women will suffer a serious depression in her lifetime. Mothers with toddlers are the most psychiatrically symptomatic group in the United States, and a woman is a much more likely to experience psychosis after the birth of a child than she would be otherwise. The challenge of having children for many women, then, lies in keeping three bright balls in the air, and one of those balls is burning: there is the child, the job, and the mind, which, I imagine, is shaped like a sphere, shadowy, full of fire, holes, and roots.

My baby was born one month early, in a bad way. My water broke, full of green gunk. There was an infection, an emergency. I was sliced open and torn up. The little girl was gorgeous.

The first few months of motherhood were so easy, it was a dream! The baby slept all the time. She was well-mannered and pinkish. I thought, "Why did I ever worry about this?" The baby had a soporific effect on me; as soon as she was in my arms, I just wanted to doze. I occasionally worried that she was autistic, because she seemed to be so much in her own world, but mostly, for me, early motherhood was more powerful than any pill in its calming, centering effects.

Soon enough, though, things changed. The baby got an attitude. She started to stand up and refuse food. Winter came. The sun set earlier and earlier, sinking down like the lopped-off head of a golden eel, and then gone. My symptoms returned. Whereas in the past, however, my obsessions had usually focused on light switches and numbers, now they focused on the child. I began to count her calories. I spent hours calculating kilos. Worried that she was losing weight, I bought a scale. Then I worried that the scale was inaccurate, so I bought a second scale. I got the idea in my mind that the baby would eat better in darkness. I don't know why I got this idea, but I started insisting on feeding her with the lights out. My husband came home one day and found us in her nursery, scarves over all the windows, a tiny silver spoon, just shining.

In the eighth month of motherhood, my doctor increased my medications. I went back to work and that helped. However, every day, driving to work, I had to pass the hospital where I spent so many years. The hospital took on a new meaning for me. It wasn't just about illness anymore. It was about separation. I pictured myself in the hospital and my daughter alone at home. One day, I parked the car in the lot and stood at the entrance for a while. Truth be told, it is quite likely that at some points during my daughter's childhood I will have to be admitted. My medicines don't always work. My illness augurs abandonments big and small. But then again, is not abandonment intrinsic to mothering? From the very moment we expel our children from the womb, we abandon them. No one is perfect. It occurred to me, standing at the entrance to the hospital, half in, half out, that my very desire for perfection, for complete control, for counting every calorie and shining every spoon, put my mothering at risk far more than any hospitalization such symptoms may cause. I decided to dance.

I went to a dance studio at the corner of our street. Maybe I was not in my right mind. Maybe I was. "I'd like to learn to tango," I said. When I was very young, I had seen a woman tango, and the image stayed with me, her limpid form, the simple spine visible beneath her black bodice. Tango requires flexibility, spontaneity, exactly what obsessive-compulsive disorder was not, and exactly what one needs to manage motherhood.

My instructor's name was Armand. He had an oiled black pompadour and slick shoes. "Doublestep, doublestep, doublestep," he'd cry as he whooshed me across the floor. Armand taught me the intricacies of tango and milonga, the drag and sweep, the circle and swirl. In the center of the circle I pictured my brain, my red-hot head, which I was dancing around, letting it flame and seize without me. Dancing was my meditation. Through it, I learned not to control my mind but to bypass it completely.

As a new mother, especially a mother with mental illness, tango has been an indispensable tool. There are many times when I am caught in the snarl of my own obsessive symptoms, my child's needs, and the regular, daily demands of life, and to navigate these currents, one needs a swashbuckling step. Let me be specific. My daughter is a year old now. I no longer worry about her food. Lately, I have been concerned with a particular pattern of stars only I can see in my ceiling. I keep needing to trace this pattern with my eyes. My brain is bad, so bad! Some people say OCD is purely neurological, a tic-like illness similar to Tourette's. I believe this. My brain seems to have the hiccups; it seizes and cramps. All day I need to count the stars in my ceiling. The worst part is, my daughter needs me, and I need numbers. "Mama, mama, mama," she calls, but I'm stuck, and then I say to myself, "Drag left, uncurl," and I picture myself doing it—uncurling—swirling between the stars, back down to where she waits, to where we live, together.

I take tango lessons twice a week for one hour. It's a spiritual practice for me, a meditation through movement. I know I am extreme; most mothers go to a gym or to a therapist for support, but I believe the difference with me is one of degree, not kind. What mother doesn't have to dance between her own needs and tugs, her child's cries, her dreams, his desires? What mother doesn't come at this most complex of projects with a handicap of some sort, somewhere? You tell me, what mother is perfect? To my daughter I say this: I am sorry. I am so far from being able to give you all that you need, but know one thing. You have my whole effort. You have my whole heart, for whatever it's worth. I love you.

Yesterday, this girl I love did something very strange. We were in her bedroom and she began to knock on the wall, for no reason I could see. I thought, "Oh god, she's going to turn out like me." To distract her, I put on a tape. It was Peter, Paul, and Mary singing about lemons. I sang too. The words wooed my daughter, and she, for the first time after a mere twelve months on this blue planet, began to dance. Tap tap. Tap tap. But these were not obsessive taps. These were good taps. Strong taps. Foot taps. Hand claps. She has beautiful rhythm.

6

My Life as a Father

The first word my daughter said was "Papa." The second word my daughter said was "Papa": this is *Papa* with a difficult *p*, not an easy *d*, not *Da-da*, everyday baby mumbo jumbo; my daughter was not speaking mumbo jumbo, she was speaking significance, the thing closest to her heart, Papa first, Papa second, and then, third, "Lila," which is the name of our thirty-pound sweet Shiba Inu dog, who somehow managed to take up a place on my child's tongue before me, the mama. "Ma ma, mama, maaa-ma," I'd say to my girl, and she'd grin back, a chip of white tooth erupting from her red gum, and refuse me. "Papa," she'd squeal. Her world, right from the start, was all about dad and dog with me on the fuzzy periphery, waving my arms around and insisting that I be seen.

Maybe I'm overstating it. My daughter loves me. She blows me *besitos*, the Spanish term for little kisses, and in grocery stores she occasionally puts her plump arms around my neck and rests the scrumptious pad of her cheek against mine, so it's like we're dancing then, waltzing one on one. My husband, Benjamin, tells me I'm being oversensitive. "Of course she loves you," he says, but we both know she loves him best. In any case, I tell myself, I deserve it. I am, after all, a modern mother, and my husband is, after all, a modern father, and this is just what I said I wanted. Two years ago, on September 28, the Clearblue test wand turned clear blue, and I made my husband, a chemist, swear on his hops vine that he'd be as active a parent as he is a gardener. He is a great gardener, spending hours in the spring sun coaxing dahlias and delphiniums from the ground while I hunch inside, staring at my computer screen, worrying over words. "We can't have this child," I'd said to him, waving the test wand in front of his face, "unless you swear you're in it with me fifty-fifty."

"Forty-sixty," he'd answered.

"No," I'd said. "It's fifty-fifty or nothing. I'm not doing sixty percent of the parenting. My career is just as important as yours."

"I mean," he'd said, "I'll do sixty percent, even seventy. You do forty, or thirty. I'm shortening my hours at work once the baby is born."

Very cool, I thought. I bragged to my friends about how cool my husband was, a real feminist who'd put his money where his mouth was; who, literally, would swallow his salary and swaddle the baby; who would, he promised me, walk his talk. All throughout the pregnancy I suspected he'd renege, but he didn't. Clara was born by C-section after a two-day labor, and I was so wiped out and drugged up that he was the first to hold her. It was he who insisted with a touching and slightly irritating enthusiasm that we take *every* class the postpartum unit offered, from feeding to first aid to bathing. Once at home, it was he who got up with the baby five nights out of the seven, he who took three weeks paternity leave while I scooted back to my office after just seven days, my cesarean scar still oozing. I was determined not to fall prey to motherhood, as though motherhood were a maw. My vision of motherhood comes, of course, from my own mother, who was more or less devoured by her children—she had four of them in close succession. My own mother never had a paying job, she drank cocktails with pitted olives speared with frill-topped toothpicks, and wept in frustration in the vast master bedroom from the hollowness of her life. I could not allow such a thing to happen to me. This wasn't the fifties; this was the nineties, and feminism, far from reappropriating the dignity of motherhood, had taught me to try to escape it, even though my ovaries were silver sacs stuffed with human eggs, and my heart, well, even while my heart, in a secret corner, could not wait to feel the flesh of my flesh, close against me.

I gave birth; he got up nights. I went back to work as a psychologist and a writer full-time; he went back to work as a chemist half-time, and something not-so-strange but difficult happened. Clara started to like my husband more. This was the first problem, and it was piercing. When the baby was nine months old, she began waking in the middle of the night from nightmares. Of course, we can't be sure they were nightmares, and if they were, I can't imagine what a nine-month-old's demons would be—maybe vague watery dreams of sharks and falling, of smothering skin. She'd scream out. We'd both bolt upright in bed. It was always dark then, with maybe a crescent moon clamped against the sky, or stars salted generously; the baby screamed. "I'll go," I'd say, throwing off the covers. "No, I'll go," he'd say, throwing off the covers. And then there was the night I heard it. "Papa!" she screamed. What happened next is obvious. Papa leapt up, ran to her room, and Mama lay alone, listening through the monitor to sounds of cooing and comforting, not made by me. Not my sounds.

I smelled a skunk on our front lawn. I remembered as a child wanting to touch a de-scented skunk in a pet store, the thick stripe of white icing on its furred black back, the delectable snout. I wanted to touch my daughter, my baby girl; it would not be too much to say I ached for it, but someone had usurped me, at my insistence. I thought of all the other times, in all the other ways, she clamored for him first. It was he who had to put on her shoes, to brush her hair, to bathe her. *Papa papa papa.* But the night of the skunk was when I fully realized how the modern mother, freed from the burden of primary-care giving, gains a lot and loses a lot, in language and in love.

Most women, in becoming mothers, feel they finally come to understand their own mother with more depth and compassion. For me, in becoming a mother, I felt I finally came to understand my father and what must have been his inevitable feelings of "fringeness," as the woman he married ran the domestic show. To be loved second best, how have men tolerated that all these years? How awful, how hurtful. It makes you want to withdraw. Now I see why fathers fade away. There is no way to compete with the fierce love a child has for its primary caretaker, and it's so easy to feel rebuffed when the little one shakes off your hand and runs for her obvious favorite. So you retreat, to your study, your den, your desk, your TV, where there is always football. At one point, early in my daughter's life, I actually started to watch football, half out of humor, half out of resignation. Men so padded they couldn't feel a thing rammed helmeted heads and tossed a rawhide sphere through the air. "What are you *doing?*" Benjamin asked me, coming into the room one day as the Patriots and Jets had it out.

I looked up. He was carrying Clara in one arm, a stack of freshly washed bibs in the other. Crowds cheered, touchdown. The baby gave him a huge, open-mouthed kiss, and something lurched in me. "I hope you washed those bibs in Dreft," I said, a detergent for very young skin.

"I didn't," he said. "I don't believe in Dreft. Tide's just as good."

"What do you mean you don't *believe* in Dreft?" I said.

Whereupon followed a long, exhausting argument about the relative merits of Dreft over Tide. This is just one of the liabilities that happens when a husband becomes the mother, the mother the father. It's sociologically complex, and the power plays perpetual. As "the primary caretaker," Benjamin feels it's within his purview to choose the detergent, the clothes, the types of diapers. While, on the one hand, I've asked him to do this, at least partially, on the other hand, I'm *a woman*; I gave birth to that baby, no one else, just me, and I secretly believe he should step aside and let me assert my innate rights over her life when I want. This leads to frequent bickering. In traditional arrangements, one parent inhabits the work sphere, one the domestic sphere, and the division of labor is not only clear but in keeping with gender. However, in our case, the gender thing is confused, and on top of that, or because of that, both of us dabble in both spheres, he a little more in one, I a little more in the other, but there is overlap. The politically correct thing to do is not always the easiest or most efficient or sanest. Having both parents mucking about in sex roles while also weighing in on detergent, binkies, and shoe size can make for pretty slow going. If I were a real football father, I'd just step out of the way, but I'm not. I'm also a mother. When Clara kisses him, calls for him over me, I feel in part resignation—*well, what the hell, I'll just watch the game*—but in part a kind of fierceness that has led me to feel ever more confused as to why so many men have for so long been willing to sit on the sidelines. As a parent, the sidelines is a radically free and lonely place to be.

My problem is, I want it both ways. I want the freedom that comes with traditional fatherhood and the closeness and primacy that comes with traditional motherhood. I want to be the center of my baby's life while I leave her for eight, nine, ten hours at a time to pursue my own central interests. I see the essential impossibility and selfishness in my desire, but even more surprising to me is that underneath my working-woman, let's-get-it-done feminism exists a real reservoir of traditionalism, even conservatism; what I call Phyllis Schlafly-ness.

For instance, a few weeks ago the baby got sick. Because we have been blessed, so far, with an incredibly robust little girl, any illness we experience as a deviance, a departure. I had been in California on a writing assignment for a few days, one of the many work-related trips I'd taken since her birth. When I got back to Boston, rain was pounding down, the taxi stunk of smoke, and I keyed open the front door of our house to find a fever-faced child lying on the couch with a dozy-looking dad. "She's got a little cold," he said to me. A little cold? The child's nose was plugged from nostril to neocortex; her breath was wheezy and her eyes had the glazed look of predelirium. I put down my suitcase. "Benjamin," I said, "she looks awful. Have you taken her temperature?"

"We don't need to take her temperature," he said. "I can feel her fever with my hand. It's about one hundred."

"A hand is not a thermometer," I said. "I'm going to take her temperature."

"No you're not," he said to me.

"*What?*" I said. "You're telling me what to do? I'm her *mother.*"

The word hung dead in the air. *Mother.*

"Lauren," he said, "it upsets her to have that rectal thing in her butt. There's no need. I gave her Motrin."

"I'm her mother," I said again and started to cry.

I was crying in part because my baby was sick, in part because I had jet lag, and in part because, at that moment, as in many others, I wanted just to be her mother and have all the prerogatives that role has traditionally enjoyed: to choose the medicine, to take the temperature, to be *in charge*, solo. Somewhere in my heart exists a trenchant traditionalism that says a "real mother" does not share the work of parenting; she hogs it; it's her special domain. And I wanted to dance there, in that domain, a real mother, cheek to fevered cheek, with my own sick girl.

After this incident I decided to change things. I'd had enough of my modern ways. I was going to quit my day job as a psychologist and spend more time with my daughter. I was going to insert myself into her heart. To be honest, I was after her love, but other things too. I was feeling competitive with her father. And I wanted to take a crack at old-fashioned caretaking, see what it felt like to claim the kind of expertise that comes only when you've spent hour upon exclusive hour watching the toddler toddle, charting the bowels, mixing the mash, *women's work*. The fact that I started to yearn for women's work shows, perhaps, just how far feminism has taken us, for what exhausted mother one hundred years ago could possibly have romanticized the difficult labor of raising a baby?

So I cut down my hours at work. This coincided with a three-week trip my husband, a chemist, was taking, the first time he'd been away from the baby since she'd been born. I couldn't wait. I felt, secretly, like *good, now we'll get him out of the way.* He left, and Clara and I were alone. It seems odd: she was over a year old now, and never had we really been alone for an extended period of time. The house was so quiet, the mornings were so yellow, the spring was so soft, the nights were so long and lush, it was blissful. Hour after unbroken hour we were together, and I experienced how a child changes time, how the moments are marked not by the ticktock of a clock but by the blurrier cycles of a baby's sleeping and waking, crying and eating; by how long a morning can be, a saffron egg yolk, the brightness of tangerine juice, the drip drip of silver drool. One year after my child was born, one week into leaving my day job, I experienced, at last, what people must mean when they say "the rapture of motherhood," for indeed it can be rapturous, and it is definitely radical, how such a small being can tip over time and make you see the tiniest thing, hour after hour, the piece of plastic on the floor, the twig, the pebble, the zigzag crack in the concrete. Like I said, there was rapture, and also revenge. Benjamin called on the phone and he said, "It's *Papa*," and she said, "*Mama*," and my heart went high up in my chest, beating both good and bad.

However, not all is so simple. Two days passed. Three days, four days. After a while, I started, sometimes, to feel bored. Well, let me be honest here. After a while, I started a lot of the time to feel bored. This is not easy to admit, and I'm in no way saying my daughter is boring but, rather, that I, as an adult with serious cerebral tendencies, lack the capacity to imaginatively enter her world on an ongoing basis. Zigzags, cracks, pebbles, and plastic are enchanting for only so long. I am sure, in this sense, I am no different from many, or most, mothers, who find the world of a baby tiring over time. But, somehow, I didn't think it would happen so soon. Or, perhaps, I found the boredom harder to tolerate because I am a person so naturally inclined towards product, whereas a baby is all process. In any case, it didn't take long before my mind was wandering back to a Trollope novel I wanted to finish. By day seven, she'd be building a tower and I'd be sneaking furtive glances at a manuscript. By day fourteen, I was propping her in front of *Sesame Street* and encouraging an Elmo obsession. By day eighteen, I had hired a babysitter for four hours and then paid her for an extra hour overtime because, well, I had a few writerly ideas I thought I might like to scribble down. By day twenty, I was singing *Papa Papa Papa*, eager for his return. Eager to go back, sixty-forty, seventy-thirty, for he, her papa, possessed caretaking talents I do not. He likes to build towers hour after hour, day after day. He likes red-wagon rides and yellow ducks. He does excellent animal imitations and knows how to toss her just shy of the ceiling while she squeals in ecstatic delight.

Benjamin returned. Not long after, I went back to work full-time because, well, I like work. It was with sadness and also relief that I came to this understanding, and that I let my husband reinsert himself into Clara's life in a major way. The sadness had to do with giving my daughter up, but it was more than that, for many parents give their child up to other caretakers. What's different in my situation is that this caretaker also happens to be my husband, not a paid outsider. And this adds a complex element to our marriage. Our marriage now has an edge of competition, a little lake of loneliness for me, and an off-kilter triangle shape that it didn't have before and for which there are few social role models. None of my women friends have this particular challenge, by which I mean none of my women friends feel like fathers in the triad of a family. None feel, as females, as mothers, left out, on the sidelines. None struggle with their husbands over the mundane details of raising a baby. They choose the binkies, the shoes, the doctors. On the one hand, I feel I am very lucky, for I am in the unique situation of being both with and without child, a paradox that, like all paradoxes, confers confusion and possibility. On the other hand, I know I have willingly lost an opportunity to be the *one and only*, the *most adored*, and my girl, well, my girl has lost the opportunity to have the close, conflicted kind of mother-bond that most daughters enter the world with, a bond full of edge, anger, and, almost always, passion.

But I am oversimplifying. My daughter, after all, blows me *besitos* and rests the scrumptious pad of her cheek against mine, not as often as I'd like, but a kiss, even air-blown, lingers on the skin for a very long time. After my three weeks solo with the baby, it is true, I have gone back to work full-time; it is true I have left my daughter physically with her father, but make no mistake about it: Clara lives in me.

Perhaps what differentiates humans from animals is their capacity to imagine. Hours and hours during the day go by when I do not think at all of Clara and then suddenly, unbidden, she leaps into my mind, and I miss her with a fierceness bred of distance. This is its own sort of passion, is it not? By the end of the day, I cannot wait to see her, my girl! I come rushing home. Yesterday, rushing homeward, I got stuck behind a funeral procession. I wanted to lean in on my horn and honk mortality away, let me through, let me through! I couldn't get through, though, so I had no choice but to trail the mourners, and I saw, after a while, that I was one of them. I miss my girl a lot. I wonder if, when I come to the end of my life, I will regret having opted out of being the primary parent, even while I know that the option connotes luxury, luckiness; most women in this country *have* to work, which means they have to turn the child care over to someone else. I also wonder, sometimes, if my marriage will survive the tilted triangle it has become. Trailing behind the mourners, being one of the mourners, I pictured myself—maudlin writer that I am—on a ridiculously overdone death bed, a powdered satin pillow under my graying head, and my girl standing by my side. What will I leave her with? Many, many things: Empty spaces. An unusual father I was selfish enough and generous enough to really let into her life. A paradoxical mother who, if push came to shove, in some big, ultimate way, would lay down her life for her—I have no doubt about that: shoot me, save her, absolutely—but who, on a daily basis, chose work pursuits. And of course, the fruit of those pursuits are these words, every one of which tells a certain story, and the story is this: I am not my mother. I have not had a hollow life. Follow me, Clara, I am trying to do for you what my mother could not do for me. I am providing you a path, etched in ink, full of spiky sounds. I hope it will help you on your way. I hope, in knowing my full life, you will be better able to shape your own. This is my way of telling you. Not the best way, but my best way. A tale. The trade-offs. The luckiness, the luxury, the difficult choices. Read them. Rewrite them, better.

7

Isosceles

Eighteen months after the birth of my first, the wand turned positive once again, the delft-blue lines unmistakable in their message. Actually, I'd known before the test; I had the tell-tale signs, the loginess, my sense of scent enhanced, so barbecue sauce, fresh snow, hot coffee, and catsup were broken down into their component parts: tang and iron, fruit and dirt.

I took the test at Pizzeria Uno, where I'd gone with my girl after an all-too-common spat with my husband. What the spat was about, I don't recall; money maybe, or *you do the dishes*, or *you work too hard*, or *you accuse me all the time*, stupid fights, dingbat fights, the sorts of fights we'd rarely had before we became proud parents, washed out, worn out, our child glowing with good health.

So there I was, at Pizzeria Uno, single pie, deep dish, the crust with that golden flake to it. And I had the box in my pocket. And I stood up and carried my girl to the girl's room, where I peed on the stick and together we watched the wash of blue saturate the window, the slow suffusion of a pretty color resolving itself into two lines, penned and indelible. My girl pointed. "Ooo," she said. "Zebra."

I hadn't planned on getting pregnant; it was an accident, as all pregnancies in some sense are. That the sperm ever reaches the celestial egg, that it ever manages to pound its way through the zona pellucida, that the egg cell splits with nary a rip, that it lodges in the uterus and flings itself towards human form; all of this is, if not an accident, certainly unbelievable, random, beyond even our best-laid preparations. As for me, there were no preparations; the diaphragm must have slipped, and the chain of coincidences that comprise humanity happened. It happened. There it was. Mother of one. Mother of two. Two! Did I want a second child?

Who doesn't want a second child? A one-child family curses itself forever into the shape of the stern triangle, all isosceles. The two-child family, though, or the three- or the four-, is where you get the stable squares, the whimsical octagons, shapes without point and problem. In our family, my daughter frankly loved my husband better than me. He was the magician; I, the administrator. He yelped and rolled and built huge snowmen with her, while I stayed inside and stocked the cupboards with Balmex and laxatives. I often felt left out of their rip-roaring cub play because I am not a cub. I am a woman. A second child, I thought, staring at the stick in that Pizzeria Uno, a second child will balance us out; one for me, one for him. Let's do it.

I put the pregnancy test, still damp, in my pocket. I took my daughter back to our table, which was situated directly under a wall sporting wooden signs with faux legends: "Farmacy," "Olde Taverne," "Psychiatrist, One flight up," with a gloved hand pointing the way. I stared and stared at those signs. I felt a wave of nausea, although, it was too early for that. It was just my imagination. Another child, to even us out. Another child, a second expression of who we were, combined. A secret. An excellent surprise.

And yet already, I had my misgivings: Money. Time. Career. The quote I'd read somewhere: "With one, you're a moving target. With two, you're a sitting duck." I felt like a duck, heavy and webbed. I felt elation and fear.

That night, at home, after I'd put my girl to bed, I said to my husband, "I'm pregnant again." He was sitting at the dining-room table doing what he always does: making molecules. He's a chemist, and in his spare time his favorite thing to do is to make model molecules out of toothpicks and marshmallows. A molecule with one added marshmallow turns Thorazine to penicillin; two added marshmallows and an antidepressant becomes speed; a molecule with six marshmallows arranged in a hexagon is estrogen; drop one, and poor progesterone emerges, the slightest shifts causing chaos in the world. Add one. Delete another. The balance is totally blown.

He put down his work. His hands were dusted with white. He looked up at me and licked one finger. "You're kidding," he said.

"No kidding," I said. I showed him the test.

"Do you want another child?" he said.

"I don't know," I said. "Do you?"

"If you do," he said.

"What do you mean, if I do? You can't put it all on me."

"Why not?" he said.

"Look," I said slowly. "I'd maybe have another kid. But only if you really, really wanted it."

"Well," he said, "I feel exactly the same way. I'd do it, but only if you really, really wanted it."

"What about money?" I said.

"We don't have enough," he said.

"We have a lot more than most," I said. "People have done it on less."

"That's true," he said.

"What about my mind?" I said. I have, after all, an impressive history of psychiatric problems; my first pregnancy had so destabilized me I'd wound up in bed most days, too weepy and frantic to go to work.

"That's a problem," he said.

"Who knows," I said. "Maybe this time I'd be okay."

In the following few days, I pursued the question like a pollster. I called relatives and friends. My friend Corinna, mother of a three-year-old and a one-year-old, said, "It's really no different having two. You're all set up already. The second one sort of slips in." But my friends Harvey and Lina said, "Two more than doubles the workload. You'll never have downtime again."

That scared me. A lot. I am, after all, a writer and a depressive, both of which require downtime for their practice. And while I say this tongue in cheek, I've experienced both my vocations—the one I chose and the one that chose me—with a ferocious intensity. Writing takes mental space; even off the page, characters are calling out, talking, assuming shapes, so the goblet of your head feels, at times, uncomfortably full, and is there room for any more? Oftentimes, with my one child, I felt the pull between the page and her extraordinary self to be too much. My study is on the third floor of our house. It sits separated by a steep staircase and veils of unswept cobwebs. In here, I do my dreaming. And yet on so many days, she finds me, makes her way up, up, bangs on the door: "Mama, I made banana bread!" "Mama, I have water balloons!" And the crusty old conflict starts again; here or there, this or that; frustration that I've been disturbed, desire to be by her side, and when her footsteps recede, relief and grief. This is the life of a working mother.

So, surely, to add another would be to uncomfortably crowd an already snug ship. And what would happen if the ship went down, if my mind went down, if the stress of a second tipped me over the ever-present edge? I consider myself a woman with a handicap, plain and simple. After five hospitalizations and two decades on a raft of medications, it's hard to see myself as anything but. I do quite well, though, so long as the seas are smooth. Pregnancy, however, is never smooth. It's a tidal surge of psychoactive hormones; it's a blitzkrieg on the brain. Many women find it pleasant, those lapping waves of estrogen. Some, like me, find it corrosive.

But then there are your dreams and models, neither of which goes lightly. Many people have, from their childhood, the formative stories, and mine were those of Gerald Durrell, who wrote a book I'll never forget: *My Family and Other Animals*. I read it when I was twelve, under the arching elm tree in our backyard. I read it breathless and full of something brimming, both at the same time. Durrell described his family by a blue Aegean sea: there were brothers and books, sisters and singing, there were artsy bohemian parents with poetry and cigarettes. And then there was my own family, or rather, my foster family, where I did my growing up: a ramshackle house with a German shepherd, six cats, two albino rabbits with the palest pink eyes, a raccoon named Amelia, mice bred for blueness, mutton chops and roasted potatoes, a garden growing purple eggplants and tomatoes red as ornaments on their strong-smelling vines; a house crowded with kids and babies and animals and fruits, shouting, instruments, dope, fecundity every-where, every one of us a practicing poet. What a situation! What a place! My foster parents read us *Macbeth* and showed us how to till the earth and taught us Latin. Their kids were strays, like me. When I thought of family at its best I thought—and still do—of my foster home and my huge-hearted foster parents, who picked children from the streets and animals from shelters and patched together something crooked, chaotic, and sweet.

Of course, I wanted to replicate this, though, unlike my foster parents and despite my unruly upbringing, my tolerance for the far flung and dissonant is minimal. But we want what it is we're not. I wanted to be the best kind of woman, penning her poems while sprinkling sugar on cookies, a house full of scat and sweetness, a woman at once corporate and chaotic, artistic and organized, immersed and transcendent. I wanted it all.

I spent the first nights of my known pregnancy with all these thoughts, the back and forth, the ambivalence of the bourgeois woman. I focused on the conundrum of the car. How, I wondered, does a woman get one infant and one toddler into two car seats? Do you put the infant on the lawn while you strap the two-year-old in? Do you tether the two-year-old to the fender while you buckle in the baby, who is, in all likelihood, screaming? It was difficult getting out of the house with one. Even going to the grocery store felt like packing for a camping trip, exhausting. Two baby bags? Two different-sized diapers? At $17.44 a box? On the other hand, two together on a snowy day, two sisters telling secrets, a scrumptious baby to bury my face in. Lovely. Awful. The only thing I could see clearly was my status as a pregnant woman, which allowed me to agonize and weigh, in my Crate & Barrel bed.

Morning came. It came in an unpleasant way, the sun slitting open the sky, the rays streaming in through the window sharp in my gritty eyes. I got up. Cold. Cold. Cold. I'd forgotten how cold one gets in early pregnancy, the uterus taking all the blood.

Downstairs: "Wake up, Clara, it's time for school."

No go. "Clara? Clara?" Her eyelids were white and shut; her chest, unmoving. Early in her life, I used to check on her several times a night, just to make sure she'd keep going. Now I yelled, "Clara!" No response.

Slowly, slowly, I lowered my hand to her heart. Even as I did it, I knew exactly what I'd find: her breath. But there is always the fear that this time she won't be there, your one and only, your best beloved, felled by some accident or disease in her sleep. And if it happened, you would not go on. This is not an idle fear. It's an everyday occurrence, how your only child heightens your awareness of risk, sharpens your love to a painful point. "Clara!" I shouted. She opened her eyes, smiled a sly little grin.

As it turned out, she simply didn't want to go to school. At two, she was already an adolescent. No, not the pink sweater. No, she wanted pants beneath the skirt, not tights, *no tights*. And then when it was time to finally head out the door, she decided to be a dog. She grabbed the dog's collar and put it around her neck. She attached herself to the leash. She insisted on walking to our car on all fours: Hello, neighbors, hello, no I am not a dominatrix mother. My daughter barked. I started our SUV. This was insane. One was definitely enough.

Our neighborhood is full of children. The days of being socially responsible appear to be over. My neighbor Jessie said to me, "We're trying again. I can't stand the thought of Maya being an only."

"You think an only's bad?" I said. *Only. Only.* What a terrible word. It implies lack, wrongness, something missing. And yet, who doesn't have something missing? Even mothers with two children, three, four, some say they'd want more if they could. The idea that a second child would fulfill you could be as misguided as the idea that, really, anything would, because life is always lived in gaps.

I turned to Jessie. We were standing in the schoolyard, waiting to pick up our kids.

"Only one," she said, repeating the words. "It's not ideal. Who will they have to share their memories?"

I watched my daughter playing in the sharp light of winter. She swooped down the silver curves of the slide. She held hands with a black-haired girl in bright-red tights. "I love you, Lily!" she yelled out. How could I deny her a built-in biological friend?

Later on, I mentioned that to my husband.

"Friend?" he said. "I never much liked my sister."

Then this happened: my husband lost his job. He has a chronic arm injury that makes computer use excruciatingly painful, and frankly, he was grateful for the layoff, a time to rest. It occurred to me, though not for the first time, that we lived in the shadow of sickness; we were both wounded, in different ways. He cannot use a screwdriver or hold a pen; I can hold a pen, for sure, but I take six pills per day. So, he was out of work, and the Dow had, at that point, started its gruesome slide. We could no longer afford our child care, which shouldn't have mattered, given that now he was home, but how could he stay home and look for employment at the same time? Money. Money. Money. Meanwhile, inside the capsule of my uterus, this being was forming, the size of a bean, with two embossed spots inked in. We calculated—how horrible—what a second would cost us, extra years of day care, high school, college. I went to the ob-gyn and heard the heartbeat. It was going so fast, like it was anxious. I started to cry.

And yet something was urging me onward, onward. Brute physiology. And the fact that once you have a child, abortion is never what it was. You've looked at all the pictures. You've seen how the flippers become fingers, how the iris is developed, how the webwork of the brain gets laid down like filaments of the palest pink. When you're twenty, you can pluck it from you rather carelessly, but when you're thirty, when you're forty, you know just what the embryonic blob becomes.

"Maybe I should just stay home," he said to me. "And be a house husband."

"You want to live off my writing," I said, my voice flat, exhausted. "I'd have to publish hundreds of pieces per year."

"You could do it," he said, his voice all jubilant. "You're really prolific. You're productive."

"Fuck you," I said. "I am not a machine. Maybe I don't want to write magazine pieces for the rest of my life. Maybe I want to write fairy tales."

"That won't put bread in our basket," he said, still maddeningly jovial.

"You want a second kid," I said, "then get off your ass and drive a UPS truck if you have to."

Our daughter looked at us, back and forth, back and forth, like she was at a tennis match.

"I don't want a second child," she said.

"You don't want a brother or a sister?" I said.

"No," she said. "I want a fox."

The actual hard-core nausea started, and the accompanying fatigue. At five p.m., I was in bed, dragged down, each nap a small, delectable death. In my first pregnancy, this had been doable, as there was no child to care for. Now, however, I had a child to care for, and I wasn't doing it well. My psychopharmacologist said, "This probably isn't such a great idea, what with your history and all." After that, my husband said, "You know, we don't need to go through with this now. I read about a woman who had a second when she was sixty-three."

Another friend said, "You could always adopt."

"Now or never," I said to my husband, because the baby was in me. In me! "You better get a job."

To his credit, he looked and looked. He looked panicked. We hired temporary child care so I could earn and he could look. We began to see ahead of us a long life of serious toil, just to make ends meet. When we were fifty-three, we'd be scratching the bottom of our savings to pay for college. It wasn't just the money. It was what the money represented, a life where you squeeze yourself out to the last drop, husked by a system that demands cash in exchange for basic needs, like health care, like education. My friend Elizabeth said, regarding money, "I'm having a second. I just figure there'll be a way to do it," and of course she was right. There's always a way to do it. But at what cost? And why rock the boat, especially when it's rickety? And, yet, to not rock the boat, to live a life only on the safe side . . . Risk and benefit. Benefit and risk. These are hard to assess even when your thinking is clear. My thinking grew muddied. The clock on the bedside table sounded strange, a rat, nibbling away at the night.

One night, late, I woke up. I was eight weeks pregnant now. Benjamin had sent out batches of CVs. He was getting worried, his face pale, his arms tensed and hurting. And I woke up, the house dense in its darkness, a single headlight sweeping over our ceiling, then gone. I turned in the bed and he was not there. I found him in his study, staring out the window. Here's what was strange. It was snowing, and the window was open, and the snow was piling up in drifts on his desk. We couldn't keep that weather out, you see. His computer was frosted, his pens furred, his hands speckled with white. "Benjamin," I said, softly. "Benjamin, close the window."

"The window's broken," he said in a soft voice, and as soon as he said that, I saw the baby recede from me; I saw the baby get very small and distant. I looked at my husband. There was something so sad and strained in his face, and in my face too, I'm sure. And it suddenly occurred to me that either way, no matter what we did, we were going to regret it. "I'm getting an abortion," I said. I said it more to see what it sounded like, to try it on, but when he turned to me, I saw something hopeful in his eyes.

"We can't have everything," he said.

Back in our bedroom, I slid open the night table. I'd put the positive pregnancy test in there, a sort of souvenir. "Zebra," my daughter had said. Now I saw the stripes as just that: stripes. Two lines. Our limits.

Research on the matter is mixed. Some say an only child risks narcissism and loneliness. Others say singletons are more mature and often become leaders. My neighbor Jessie is nine months pregnant now, and she is sure of her way: "I want my daughter to have family when we die." So do I, oh, so do I! And yet this is what we decided: we are a family, a thorny, three-sided family that, like any business or organism, must know how far it can grow. What are the resources: internal, external? What are you willing to risk for the sake of growth? At what point do your gifts to your child become her liabilities as well, for, if we had a second who added so much stress that we weren't able to be good parents, then what in the end was she gaining? A sibling to take care of her? A sibling to take care of? These were the things we started slowly to see.

I had an abortion at eight weeks, and I am not proud to say that, god no, not at all. But I needed to protect what was definitely human, at the expense of that which was not. Soon after the abortion, the fatigue and depression ebbed as my hormones returned to normal, my hopefulness returned, and my self emerged again, hello. Good-bye. Today, two years later, I often wonder what that embryo would have been—boy or girl, brown or blue eyed, a cuddle bug or standoffish? Either way, I would have loved it, this I know to be true. But would my marriage and my mind have survived the strain of a second; would I be writing fiction as well as my more marketable magazine pieces; would Clara know how to read and write, skills she acquired early, because of the attention she has gotten? I don't say these things to make it all sound okay. It's not okay. Something serious was lost. And something serious would have been gained. An opportunity missed, but a space kept reasonably safe. We are a family that works the way we are.

Yesterday, I was with my daughter at the zoo. The white lion had just given birth, and her nipples were prominent and pink. "Why does she have so many of those?" my daughter asked.

"Because other animals have so many children, they all need a teat to drink from."

She looked down at her own chest, covered in a coat. "I have two little breasts," she announced. "Does that mean I'll have two kids?"

"Do you want two kids when you grow up?" I asked.

"I want four daughters," she said.

My heart felt heavy. "Do you wish I had more daughters for you?" I said. Leading the witness, I know. I do it all the time. How else to know what's on her mind?

"Maybe," she said. "But I'd also like a video."

"You want to watch a video tonight?" I said. "A special treat?"

She nodded, big grin.

And so we did. We watched a video about how the earth began, the big bang, the silver scarf of our galaxy, my girl nestled close in the crook of my arm. I could feel her steady breath, I could see the stars. Downstairs came the smell of my husband's cooking. On the screen, a planet was born in a milky swirl of blue. My girl said, "Mama, will my breasts make a sound when they grow?" I laughed and laughed. She's three now, my one and only. Often she says things that make me feel so delighted, a swift swish of pure happiness, that we are the way we are, a triangle, a single sail, one half of a diamond, almost precious; this solid and difficult shape.

8

Squared Off

In May of 2001, I wrote an essay for *Elle* magazine explaining why I would only have one child. In this essay I described my rather wrenching decision to abort my second pregnancy, a decision based on solid common sense: lack of finances, lack of time, lack of personal and emotional resources, a marriage already strained to its breaking point, a commitment to career. This second pregnancy occurred when my daughter was very young. I made a firm decision at that time to parent only one.

Now, years later, from where I sit, high in my house's attic, typing up these words, I can hear the caterwauling of my secondborn, produced from a third pregnancy. At six months old he has a head covered with the fine nap of blond fuzz and hands that look like a sage's. His name is Lucas. He should not be here. He should be wherever it is the pre-birthed people live, in a sea of swarming atoms, or high, high up in the air, near Jupiter.

Despite all the common sense, the careful thought, the agonizing decision, the definitiveness of the door closed on whether or not to have another child—despite it all, I went against my better judgment and, two years after the abortion, I did it. I did it just as I rounded the bend into my fortieth year. I did it as my periods started to lighten and the skin began to look crumpled around my eyes. I did it after I bit into an apple one summer morning and heard the sharp crack of a splitting tooth; I did it in decline. I did it because of decline. I did it holding close to myself the image of me and my husband as old, old people (if we are lucky enough to get that far) and the thought of who would be there for my daughter when we died. I did it as a strike against death, but more importantly than that, I did it because, in the very end, having one, for me, was just too risky.

After forty-eight hours of grueling labor, Clara Eve was born in 1999. I don't think I loved her right away. She was a truly beautiful baby, with interesting cheekbones and a mouth like a little red bow. She slept deeply. I kept thinking, *She's mine she's mine she's mine*, but she didn't feel like mine. She didn't feel like someone else's either. She felt otherworldly, as though she were surrounded by stars.

I recalled, during those days of recovery in the hospital, reading that there had been a study, or maybe several studies, showing how mothers instinctively recognized their babies by smell. If you put a new mother in a roomful of babies, according to the study, her nose would take her lickety-split to her progeny, and vice versa for babies. If you gave a newborn baby milk-soaked rags from her mother and milk-soaked rags from another mother, the baby would always put her mouth right up to Mom's, closing around the cloth, drawing in and down. These studies haunted me. While still recovering from my C-section, I would visit the hospital nursery, where troops of babies, all in blue-striped hats knotted at the top like gnomes, slept in plastic bassinets. I remember walking from crib to crib, trying to guess, or smell, which baby was mine. I purposely did not look at the nametags. All the babies seemed exactly the same to me. Maybe it was just my bad luck, but every one of them had the exact same color hair and hands that were indistinguishable from one another. All their mouths were adorable. All slept intensely, as though dreaming of the place they had left. My heart would quicken, there in that nursery, and I would peer and peer and, at last, pick a baby, the one I believed to be mine. I played this horrid little game many times. I picked my baby maybe one-quarter of the time, and the rest of the times I picked someone else's baby, and it was with dismay that I would focus my eyes on the bassinet nametags: Jack, Mary Lou, Annabelle, Galileo. Where was my girl, Clara Eve? Oh, there she was! Two rows over. Either the nurses had washed her fragrance away, or there was something seriously wrong with my nose.

And so the story goes. You know what happened with my first-born. I took her home, and time passed, and clocks ticked, and days folded into nights spent rocking and feeding. Her cries were singular, the only ones I'd heard, and she started to smile, and she started to haul herself up by holding the edges of things, and I came to love her. I fell in love with my baby girl when she was just about eight months old. I fell hopelessly, horribly, dangerously in love. She was reaching up to grasp the rims of whatever she could find, pulling herself unsteadily to her tiny feet, and I saw, then, I saw with total clarity how from this point on her world would be full of sharp points and hard floors and so many dangerous angles. This sense, that my child is in danger, has not abated over the years. Perhaps this is what mother love is. Perhaps I have finally entered into instinct. The older my child gets (she is five now), the more ferociously I worry about her, and there are sharp shards everywhere. The one thing I absolutely could not bear would be to lose her or have her hurt. And precisely because this is so unimaginably horrible to me, I spend an obsessive amount of time trying to imagine it. The world is now a series of distinct, personal flesh threats. When the children were taken hostage, and then killed, in Beslan, Russia, in 2004, I spent as much time trying to imagine what it was like for the parents to suffer such a total loss as I did imagining the terror inside that gym, where bombs were put into basketball hoops.

I attribute my decision to have a second child, in part, to terrorism. When I wrote "Isosceles," when I had that first abortion, the planes had not been taken. We didn't know what the world was. We were blind Americans. Then we saw our blindness. It's not only that

I'm afraid my child will be the victim of a terrorist act—though, of course, I worry about that—it's more the sense that I now see the world stripped of its pretense. I see that we are all still primitives living on Pleistocene plains; I see that we are slaves to rage and greed. I see that we have weapons, that we are tool builders, that we hunt and are hunted, and that even sleeping in trees will not save you. While I've always "known" this, it became glaringly obvious to me on September 11, and its obviousness grew with time.

Having a first child was not an instinctive act for me, just its opposite. But having a second? In the end, I had to do it. I did it out of raw, primitive terror and the age-old threat of loss. My own hypothesis—utterly untested—is this: the drive to have a first baby varies from person to person, but the drive to have a second, as a means of protecting yourself against loss and your child against loneliness, that is where pure biology begins to play its role. If you have a first, not having a second will always seem sad and dangerous. But if you never have a first to begin with, then you're free and clear.

When I got pregnant with Lucas, I tried to talk myself out of it at first. I tried to think it through rationally, although rationalism is not a strength of mine. I thought about overpopulation and dwindling food sources and global warming. I thought that this was not my second pregnancy; it was my third. The second one I had aborted, and what was different now? The truth is, everything was different. In between having the abortion and having Lucas, I had come, finally, to really know mother love and to understand that the world around me was gobbling up its citizens with ferocious speed. These two facts made my initial qualms seem almost irrelevant. We didn't have the money? Never mind. My marriage was already stressed? Too bad. Let's go. I tried to get pregnant; I did it on purpose, and it worked right away. We were blowing up Afghanistan and Iraq. While all over the globe bombs were falling and people were ripped up, I did what the human race does in such situations. I had sex. Two weeks later I began throwing up. My husband and my doctor said it was all in my head. No one gets nauseous so soon into a pregnancy. But I did. I didn't even have to take a test. I knew

I was having my second. I was sick for eighteen weeks, retching, de-hydrated, anemic, and not once did I seriously think of aborting it. I ate only watermelon.

This is not to say I wasn't ambivalent. I was. It's just that the ambiva-lence did not have the strength of the fear that propelled me forward. Nevertheless, especially during the eighteen weeks of vomiting, I thought, *What have I done? What am I doing?* One night my husband said to me, "We were happy with one. We don't know if we'll be happy with two. We don't know if we're strengthening or weaken-ing our family." He said this to me just as we were getting ready for bed. Our room is blue-violet in color. It has a single skylight cut in its sloped ceiling, and on clear nights you can see planes swim-ming like sharks across the sky and the javelin sharpness of stars. "We might not be happy with two," I said while above me a jet glided in its ascent. "But," I said, and then I couldn't think of how to go on. We turned out the light. *Happy happy happy*, I thought. We live near an air force base. The fighter planes are trim and dart around. They lean in on one wing like a gymnast showing off skills. They occasionally nose down and then zoom up and then disappear, leav-ing behind only their echoing roar. *Happy happy happy*, I thought as the fighter planes went by. I couldn't sleep. The baby was hanging off my heart. It hurt. I understood, then, that happiness was not a primary drive. Our Constitution got it wrong. We didn't want to be happy. We wanted to extend.

I grew enormous with my second child. I gained eighty-eight pounds. It was disgusting. It was unreasonable. I swear, for the first eighteen weeks I ate only watermelon. But it was as though my body knew to plow forward, to pack on protective fat; by the thirtieth week, even my face was huge. I looked nothing like myself. My hus-band and I went to see a lawyer. His name was Frank Grimaldi, which sounded grim, ominous to me. We went to set up wills. We hadn't thought to do this with our first, but now it was as though we'd deepened into another level of parenthood; we couldn't fake it anymore. With one, you can retain aspects of a child-free life. With two that becomes impossible. You are sucked into a stream of Gracos and Huggies and ant farms. So we set up wills.

I was eight months pregnant, and the lawyer peered at me suspiciously from his desk chair. "Who will be the guardian?" he said. We thought and thought about that: My siblings—too crazy. Ben's sibling—didn't like kids. At last, we decided on our longtime, live-in babysitter.

Two weeks later the wills came in the mail. I opened them up. It was a little like reading my own death certificate; I could smell death everywhere. The babysitter was thrilled. The night I received my will, I lay with my daughter on her bed, in her yellow room, my bulging belly pressed against her back. *I am lying with my two babies*, I thought, and then I fell asleep.

On January 20, 2004, Lucas was born via C-section. They carved him out of me and held him up, blood speckled and snuffling. He was just about ten pounds, full of himself, secure in the knowledge that he belonged here—right from the start. We brought him home on the coldest day of the year, when the air was cracking and painful, the trees black and thin. My husband said as we were in the car, the two children in back, "Well, now we're really a two-kid family," and I could hear several things in his voice: happiness, hesitancy, fear. At every rut in the road, my wound sparkled with pain. I was high on Dilaudids and had that postpartum weepiness, a mood that amplifies the meaning of everything, so you are at once full of rapture—I have a son! I have a second child!—and also full of despair.

Eventually, the vicissitudes of my mood evened out. Slowly, I got to know Lucas. My daughter displayed zero jealousy, which made me think she'd shoot up a playground someday. The winter eased and the air began to smell like spring. Walking with Lucas in his sling outside, stepping over the wet spots in the road, my cuffs splattered with mud from speeding cars, I thought of what people had said to me regarding my reason for wanting a second. "You won't ease your worry," they'd said. "You will only double it. With a second you'll have two to possibly lose."

And in some ways these rational, thoughtful friends and family members were right. Lucas came down with a strange illness; his throat was full of white spots. He screamed and screamed. Worrier that I am, I immediately assumed the worst: Small pox. Measles. Death. These fears were in no way easier to bear because I had my girl. No. I took Lucas to the doctor, and they diagnosed him with hoof-and-mouth disease.

He's better now. At night I feed him and I can feel the fontanel hardening, the plates of bone growing together in his skull. Perhaps because my daughter primed me, I fell for him more quickly than I did for her, say around week three. I feed him and I press my lips to the fading soft spot, and I see the place in his head where his pulse bubbles up. My boy. I hold him close, and it is never close enough.

Though in some ways I've doubled my worry, I feel I have also eased it in a way too primitive for words. Let me be clear: if I lost either one of my kids, especially if they were hurt in the process, it would be devastating. But now I know I would have to live through it, for the other one. And when I see Clara playing with her brother, I think it was worth it, because she truly is less alone in the world. Yes, we have less money. Yes, we cannot afford a house in a nicer neighborhood or a private school; yes, I have lost whatever remnants of the child-free life I once had. I have become exactly the kind of woman I said I would never be.

With two, in love with two, responsible for two, I have at long last set my beloved friends aside. I have no social life. Eating out almost always means the pizza place just down the road—Bertucci's. But somehow the world feels a little bit more right to me. A gap has been closed. My girl has another. And we're now four dots on some screen, the lines connecting them into a solid square. And as it turns out, my eggs are not in the same basket; I have two eggs, and they're each in their own separate spots, hatching, growing up, all around them the dangerous, smoking world. I hold my children's hands. I did not know it was possible to love so thickly. My life has in some ways been narrowed by sheer fear and flailing instinct. I have less and I have more. What matters most is this: I have absolutely no regrets.

9

The Other Mother

Before my first child was born, I knew I would need help. Even with the sixty-forty or seventy-thirty split between my husband and me, I knew assistance would be required, especially because, as time went by, that split dissolved, not all at once, but slowly, like sugar corroding a tooth. Cavities opened up, empty spaces, requiring that someone step in. Work came back to claim my husband and love came forward to claim me. Love takes time and resources and tactics, and that's why I knew I needed help.

Given my precarious mental state, I already had help, a doctor with ink-black hair and a massive desk and a thick prescription pad he wrote on with a flourish. Though he had been enough before I had my first, I now saw that I needed a different sort of support, someone in-house, someone who knew how to sew, perhaps, or draw a warm bath or pat the baby on the back. I needed . . . I needed . . . a nanny. I hate the word "nanny," smacking as it does of British privilege. I also hate the word "babysitter," because it always conjures for me the image of a woman sitting on a baby. I could say I hired "help," but that has an antebellum sound, snotty and antiquated. I hired another mother. Yes. This is exactly what I did. It was a decision based at once on total necessity—both my husband and I were back to working full-time—and also rooted in a deep sense of my own inadequacy. Though not quite admitting it to myself, I was pretty sure that whoever took the job would be so superior to me that I would step to the sidelines while she took center stage. In a sense, I would be the other mother, offering help, holding out tissues, while the real drama went on without me.

I didn't want it this way, especially because I had come to adore my daughter, but adoration does not come with built-in confidence, of which I possessed, as a mother, very little. From my own mother I had learned . . . very little. I believed, I think, that my childhood had destined me to be an anemic sort of parent, lacking in essential instinct. When I look back into my past, I often cannot even see her face, my mother's face, muffled by mist and then suddenly, swiftly appearing, like the sun burning brightly on an otherwise cloudy day, an instant of saffron brightness, and then gone. Gone! Who had been there, then? In truth, I was one of those kids raised on babysitters, so hiring one seemed absolutely natural to me. I was raised on the knees and by the sides of hired help. Corita taught me to sew; Jane nursed me through my illnesses; Angela, the Irish nanny, with hair the color of apple cider and a lilting way to all her words, Angela taught me to ride a bike, to pray (Our Father, who art in heaven, hallowed be thy name), and to name the wildflowers, things I still do today, by instinct or, rather, by habit, echinacea with their bulging centers, columbine in the woods, the purple spikes of chive, and the weedy strawflowers that rise from the ground in August. In fact, yesterday, I went to the woods with my daughter, and we named the wildflowers, studying their leaves and their corollas, and it was Angela who was there, in spirit, my own mother nowhere near.

And I was my mother's daughter, of course, similarly stunted, serrated, and rageful. My mother, her fists, her hitting. My father had told us that before my mother had children she was "a different woman, really," but the pressures and conflicts of motherhood had done her in, changed her irrevocably and for the worse. Indeed, early photographs show my mother smiling on a Cape Cod beach with a red scarf around her wind-blown hair; by the time my sister, her first, came along, her face had narrowed, her eyes small and fierce, screwed into her skull. I never knew exactly why having children caused her undoing, her mad chatter and terrible violence, but not knowing made it all the more potent, more possible.

"You are the most like your mother," my aunts always told me, ominous indeed. In order to avoid her female fate, I got a doctoral degree, published pounds of books, acquired prizes. I studiously avoided anything maternal, claiming a mannish incompetence, an inability to do baby talk and all of its equivalents. On the other hand, I held onto a sliver of hope, and my babies were born on this sliver.

Our first nanny did not work out. She came to us three weeks before my daughter was born. She was only nineteen, whip smart but boy crazy. Within a few weeks of her job she met a man, got engaged, broke up, and then got engaged to someone else. Therefore, she was, of course, preoccupied, all this yes and no, back and forth. My husband and I had no specific complaints—she didn't shake our baby or leave her thirsty—but there was something distracted in the sitter's eye, something rushed in her ways. She could barely wait for five o'clock, at which point she would race out of the house, rouge swooped onto her cheeks and her bitten lips bright with carmine. We didn't have to decide a thing. Within a month or so she left us, a white wedding gown over her arm, on her way to Pocatello, Idaho, to walk the aisle with a man she met over the Internet.

Our second nanny, Ceci, came to us from a friend of a friend of a friend of a friend. She was thirty-six—an excellent age, we thought—new to this country, with shoe-polish-shiny black hair and a beautiful face. She spoke very little English. Not long after she started, our newborn baby got sick. Clara corkscrewed her body and screamed. Her stomach felt hard and lumpy. We stretched her, thumped her, cycled her little legs, but still she screamed, her tiny tongue extended.

I remember one night when I'd been up with her until the daylight came. Ceci was living with us in a room down the hall. The baby howled. I turned on the fan to block the sound so Ceci could get some sleep. The baby yowled, one long painful skein of sound; it just went on, and on. There is really nothing like being with a screaming baby dead in the middle of the night. Her room was lit by one small bulb, shedding shadows so that my hand looked huge raised between the light and the wall. I held up the baby, and she too looked huge, her mouth a flapping, monstrous thing, her arms like wings, going nowhere.

At five in the morning, when I hadn't caught a wink of sleep, it started to get light outside. The air got grainy and gray, the lawns visible, veiled with dew, and far in the distance a radio tower blinking its red light on and off, on and off. I started to cry right along with my daughter. Perhaps I cried even louder than she, for Ceci heard, and came to get us. Mussed and sleepy, she said, "Here," and held out her arms. I gave her the baby. She said, "Go get me some lettuce leaves," which I did. She then ran a warm bath and told me to drop the lettuce leaves in. The water turned pale green; the leaves looked like lily pads, charming. She lowered my daughter in. "In our country," she said, "we know if you put lettuce leaves in a warm bath, it calms the child down." I thought this was sweet and very lyrical. Lettuce leaves! Who knew what other neat herbal cures lay in wait for us, delivered fresh from her Mexican culture—a bath of apple blossoms, a cup of hot pomegranate juice? I have never been a big believer in anything outside of Western medicine. But let me tell you this: Presto. The baby quieted down. A cynic would say it was the water, not the lettuce leaves. Who cares? She quieted down, and soon after, she fell asleep. From that day on, Ceci made our colicky daughter a bath of lettuce leaves, and from that day on the other mother, she took my baby in and always, always knew exactly what to do. She had a gift.

It did not take long for Ceci to become famous in our neighborhood. Everyone wanted a piece of her. She was too good to be true, but let me tell you, she was true, the real deal, the best. It was not so much what she did—although she did a lot—but more who she was, her competence mixed with kindness, her sheer energy. In the five years she worked for us, she never once was late for work. She never took a sick day. Amazing. But perhaps she is best described by what she did outside of her working hours. Ceci took kickboxing, English as a second language, cooking classes. She was a gifted photographer and painter. She had her degree in marketing from the University of Mexico, but her interests leaned more towards the arts. She knit elaborate blankets, used a loom, could crochet a piece of intricate filmy lace. She found a beat-up bike in the trash and single-handedly restored it to working order. She loved jigsaw puzzles, huge four footers with thousands of scrambled pieces, and she had the patience to put it all together, day after day, until a coherent scene emerged. Once she was finished, she would spray her creation with clear glue, hang it whole on the wall. It always delighted my daughter, the image at once cracked and solid, a seeming impossibility, but there it was.

I could go on. She was from a close family in a small town and had come to the States to learn the English necessary for her career. The oldest of five children, the only girl, she had been both a daughter and another mother to her siblings from her own youngest years. She was full of mystical folk cures but also common sense to the extreme. Once, my daughter had a high, high fever. She thrashed and muttered and tore at the air with her hands. I, new to all this, did not know what to do. My hands shook and I could not measure out the medicine. Ceci took the bottle from me, drew the liquid up, grasped my thrashing daughter's chin, and squirted her mouth full of cherry, all in one seemingly seamless move.

Months passed. The presence of Ceci in our family was like a light but firm hand arranging our shape in ways we could only see in retrospect. She was shocked to find out my husband and I celebrated neither Christmas nor Chanukah. My husband had been raised rigorously atheistic and anticapitalistic. I am Jewish by birth, but once I left my mother to live in a foster home, I soon lost touch with my family, and its traditions, for good. "No tree?" Ceci said that first year she was with us. "No presents? El niño. What about el niño?"

"Clara doesn't care," I remember saying. "She's only one."

"Clara cares," Ceci said. And that afternoon she came home with a tree, tinsel, a plastic star, all those silk globes. My husband looked uncomfortable, but then after a second, he smiled. By the week's end we were all zooming around town, buying up toys and trinkets, festive bows, shiny wrapping paper. "I'm Jewish," I kept saying to my husband; "I'm a communist," he kept saying to me. Then we shrugged. We were on a roll, and loving it. On Christmas Eve, Ceci took us all to Mass in a tiny basement church in the inner city. The priest was bedecked in some kind of crown and glossy robes, waving his incense stick so the whole church filled with the smell of frankincense and myrrh. Clara could not take her eyes off the princely looking priest or the children in the choir, all of whom were dressed in bright red ruffles and whose ears were pierced with tiny hoops of gold. Music started playing, something salsa-ish, and then a clip-clop hip-hop version of "Deck the Halls," and before we knew it the whole church was dancing, skipping after the skipping priest, who waved his wand of smoke high and low. We skipped too. The air was so thick and cloying I could barely breathe. I felt I would choke. On the other hand, it was a lot of fun.

It was for reasons like these that I felt enormously grateful to Ceci and continuously lucky to have her; she brought humor into our tight little lives. However, I also know that her confidence and kindness, the charm she had for children, her easy engagement with them, and her steadfast love of the things I did not love—the dressing, the hair combing, Chuck E. Cheese's, and swimming pools—only deepened my belief in my own inadequacies. I allowed it to. I felt I simply could not compare.

Here is a scene: It is early morning, and Ceci is brushing my daughter's hair. She draws the bristles through in a single sweep, hefts up a skein of the champagne-colored locks, and braids them, her fingers flying. Moments later, Clara is ready for school, immaculate, clothes matching, her hair a complex series of plaits and twists all miraculously held to her head with only a single bright barrette. Later on, after school, I find Clara in her room and tentatively approach her. My own hair I have always worn in a mop, too busy for conditioners, just a quick scrub and a brisk, business-like rinse. "Let me do your hair," I say. I say it softly, shyly, almost like I am in seventh grade asking a boy to dance. "Why?" she says. She doesn't look up. She's playing with a doll. "Because," I say, and I don't know how to go on. I pick up the brush with its flat-paddle handle and, standing over my daughter's head, I see the pink seam of her scalp where Ceci has perfectly parted her hair. I bring the brush to it, drag down, and my daughter screams. She gives a loud, dramatic murderous yell and operatic tears fill her eyes. All I did was one tiny tug. I know, I *know* I haven't hurt her. I stand there with the brush, frozen. She eyes me warily. I eye her right back. Then I cautiously slip from her room.

It is winter, shredded snow falling everywhere, muffling the mountains, bandaging the winding slopes, the skiers in their bright-red parkas looking, from a distance, like tiny beads of blood sliding down. I am twelve. I am full of holes. From across the kitchen, my mother snarls at me for reasons I cannot understand. Suddenly, she flings a spoon in my direction; it bounces off my cheek and lands, clattering, on the tiled floor.

Two years later we will sit together, my mother, father, and I, in a social worker's office on the second floor of a psychiatric unit, where I have been temporarily placed, much to my relief. My mother's left hand is badly bruised from where she put it through a wall. I, too, have various bruises, although the real problem, the relentless decimating daily humiliations, is harder to describe. The social worker tells me I will not be going home. My mother, who has become psychotically paranoid over the years, says, "You have abused me past what I can manage," a classic example of projection. I nod, not knowing what else to do. Precipitating my removal from the home was the fact that my mother tried to push me down a gorge in Vermont. I survived, saved by the soft snow. I remember standing where I had slid, hearing the sound of her receding footsteps in the forest, tasting the cold on my tongue. I was fourteen then and had just begun to bleed. The trees were black, scarred. I saw them, and I understood that my mother wanted to kill me, that she always had. What was different, today, now, post-push, was that I wanted to kill her too. This, I saw, was what it meant to be a daughter, a mother. It is about blood and all the steep slopes.

Children are not subtle. They throw their arms around you or haughtily turn away. They answer you or don't. My daughter is no different. At the end of every day, during Ceci's tenure with us, I would come home from work. My briefcase was always bulging, my mind cramped, my stomach aflutter from all I had left to do. I was, at that point in my life, working full-time as both a psychologist and a writer. I sometimes worked sixty hours a week, trying to outrun my history, building walls with words.

I remember one homecoming in particular, not because it was better or worse, but simply because a single memory becomes emblematic, standing in for all the rest. It was winter, and when I opened the door a cold gust of air blew in. Ceci and Clara were absorbed in a book, Clara on Ceci's lap, Ceci rocking the chair back and forth in time with the Spanish sentences. I could hear the words—*leche, bebé, perro*—but I did not understand. I saw my daughter's sleepy eyes, how Ceci held her. "Hi," I said, an interruption. Ceci smiled, beckoned me forward. Once she had brought me a beautiful blue vase from Mexico, and after my mastectomy, Ceci had filled my room with fresh flowers, helped me with my bandages. Now, I knelt down. "Hi, Clara," I said, holding out my arms. Clara looked at me. "Go," Ceci whispered, giving her a little push. "*Besitos para mama.*" Obediently, my daughter came forward and gave me a quick kiss.

Lest it be misunderstood, I love my daughter. I love her with my whole damaged heart. Her face has always filled me with a sense of the miraculous, for it is a beautiful face, fair-skinned, green-eyed; her limbs are lithe; she seems the expression of all that could be good in me, all that I have that is healthy. At night I often dream of my daughter. We are carrying flowers towards each other, big armfuls of fragile lupine.

Years passed this way. Clara spoke Spanish before she spoke English, and when Ceci's friends came over they laughed and remarked, "She sounds just like a little Mexican," my blonde-haired, green-eyed girl. Even so, I had moments with Clara, many moments, that were easy and unfettered, moments writing poetry together, a story called "Ick I'm Sick," discussions about stars and god, Linnaeus and reptiles. We bought a vinegar-propelled rocket and shot it together, our heads tipped back as it nosed straight into space. But her first love was not for me. Her first love was for her father, and when it came to women, her first love was, in truth—is this the truth?— for Ceci, and while I really grieved that, I also understood that I had set it up that way, a safe distance, space between mother and daughter, this dyad dangerous, rife with rejection, sick. And yet, it hurt my heart. It hurt my chest, my breasts. When Clara was three years, they found my ducts were crammed with cancerous cells. I had both my breasts removed, tiny, squishy saline bags slid into the sagging spaces left. In clothes I looked fine, but naked I looked maimed. Ceci, on the other hand, was whole and healthy. I know my daughter knew that. Sometimes she would come to me, pull down my shirt, peer in. "Ceci has nipples," she would say. "And you don't." I'm sure this was just a statement of brute fact, but I could not help hearing it as more.

And so we went on. My husband, I hesitate to say, did not help the situation. He sided with Ceci, unconsciously, subtly, giving her his credence and confidence. For this I have not decided whether or not I will forgive him. Of course, I am largely to blame, for I had impressed upon him my image of myself: the ratty foster child, the progeny of insanity, the work a defense against it all. At one point my second-born developed a pustule-like rash on his tongue and palms. Ceci hypothesized an immune response due to a recent fever. My husband agreed. They stood in the kitchen talking together while I watched from the sidelines, and they decided that if it got any worse, they would call the doctor tomorrow. *Give it a day*, they said. "Are you kidding me?" I said. "It's on the *tongue*." I called the doctor immediately. "My child has white oozing spots on the tongue," I said. *My child*. The pediatrician diagnosed hoof-and-mouth disease. For me, this was a twisted triumph.

Clara started pre-school. Here is where things took a distinctly downward turn. At the end of the day, while I was still at work, Ceci would pick her up and take her to a museum or to Chuck E. Cheese's, and bring her home at five. Eventually this became common enough that Ceci no longer needed to tell us her plans ahead of time. Autumn turned into winter. One day, their usual arrival time of five o'clock passed, and they hadn't come home. Ceci had been with us nearly four years then. The afternoon ticked on into evening. Where were they? Cars rumbled by on the road outside my study, but none of them stopped. The day grew dark. Frantic, I called my husband at work. "Clara and Ceci aren't here," I said, and I think I heard just the tiniest pause before he said, "They're fine." I called the school. It was closed. The church bells gonged. I thought crazy thoughts about Ceci: *How do I know who she really is? Would she kidnap my girl? Of course not, dummy! But how can I know?* And indeed, how could I? We had hired her years ago, based on a reference check and gut. It suddenly seemed careless, negligent; I pictured telling detectives, "She comes from Mexico," but not being able to say more. Hometown? "*Cool-ya-can?*" Something like that. Address, copy of passport, visa, we had none of it. On a deeper level, I realized we knew almost nothing of her. Her plans, her hopes, her fears, her lovers, her enemies, nothing. We knew Ceci intimately, day after day, year after year, we knew her laugh, her voice, her hands, her hair, and yet we knew her not at all. This, I believe, is common.

At six o'clock I heard a key in the lock, the dogs barking, and when I raced downstairs I saw them standing together, mittened-hand-in-mittened-hand. "Where were you guys?" I said. I was nearly wheezing with panic.

"Field trip," Ceci said.

"Field trip?" I said.

"To Foss Park. I chaperoned. It was fun, wasn't it, Clara?"

And Clara looked up, smiled, nodded. "Fun," she said.

"But I didn't . . . You didn't tell . . ." And then I stopped. I held tight to the banister. "Wait a minute," I said. "Aren't parents supposed to sign a permission slip before their kids go on a field trip?"

"Yes," said Ceci, and if she thought her next comment was strange, she betrayed it not a bit. "I signed that slip weeks ago," she said.

I did what any woman at once indebted and enmeshed would do. I said not a word to Ceci. The next day I called the school. "All permission slips," I said to the teacher, "must be signed by me. Not Ceci. Me." I paused. The teacher didn't say anything. Her silence sounded accusing. Where was I at the end of every day, during pickups? Working. Working. Working. Where was I? "I'm Clara's *mother*," I said, and I heard it echo down the line.

When I became pregnant with Lucas, Ceci, who had lived with us for four years, moved out. She found a fantastic apartment in Harvard Square, just minutes away. It was not a big change. She left most of her clothes, her bed made, her pictures up on the walls. "What are we," I said to my husband, "a storage facility?"

"You're just jealous," he said.

"Picture it," I said. Suddenly, I was speaking slowly, newly aware of an anger. "Picture it. You and I have a child. We hire another man to move into the house and be the nanny. Your child falls in love with the man-nanny, this other father. I come to love the other father too, and I listen to all his child-rearing advice."

"I don't listen to all her child-rearing advice," he said.

"If I think she has an ear infection and has to go to the doctor and Ceci doesn't, you always agree with Ceci."

"I'm just being polite," he said. "She's still a guest. You're my wife."

"Exactly," I said. "That's exactly my point. I'm your wife. I'm Clara's mother."

"Clara loves you a lot," he said.

"Of course she does," I said.

"You have to have more confidence," he said.

"You tell me," I said, and I was surprised by the depth of my anger. "You tell me how you would feel having another father around for your kid."

"I would hate it," he said thoughtfully. "It is something I would never allow."

It was full-blown winter when I gave birth to my son, the trees splashed and mottled, my newborn's face patchy with different hues of reds and blues. When I looked into his brand-new face, I saw nothing of my mother and nothing of myself. In part because of gender, in part because of experience, I approached my second with much more confidence, lifting him up by his armpits, swaddling him deftly, bathing him both swiftly and softly, and he felt it, my calm hands. He stopped crying whenever I picked him up. I picked him up as often as I could. Ceci seemed to like him less. "Boys," she'd say and sigh. "Girls are fun," she'd say. "The clothes . . . Boys are . . ." And then she wouldn't finish. From his earliest days Ceci dressed him in little baseball shirts and high tops. She called Clara "*mi amore*" and Lucas "señor." "It's a cultural thing," my husband said. "It's Latino machismo." Sometimes she let Lucas cry and cry. "Oh," Ceci said to me one day. "Oh, he is a big bad boy. He has a terrible temper." At the time, Lucas was two months old.

I see this gender bias as one of Ceci's unintentional gifts to me, for it left a space, and I slipped in. I held my boy. I called him "*mi amore*." He grabbed my nose, felt my face. I know he saw me, looming large over him, as someone safe. And I learned, from him, that I was safe, that I was not my mother, that I did not have claws or cruelty, that I could never hurt a child, my children, never, never, ever, girl or boy, no matter, these were indeed my children. My life. The best I had to offer.

Every child changes you in different ways. Clara curved me towards my past and, in doing so, forced me to consider its complex intersection with my present curving relentlessly towards my future. Lucas revealed for me the beauty of the single dimension. As a writer, unidimensionality is something I have always avoided. The worst thing that could be said about one's work was that it lacked facets, was flat. Clara and I are two pieces of a single prism that keeps catching the light at an infinite number of angles. With Lucas, the surface is smooth. It is smooth, peaceful, a lake without wave or ruffled ripple, a lake whose very depth is implicit in its liquid skin. I could float here, catch my breath. I sang silly songs to him:

His name is Lucas
Lucas Palookas
And he's the best
Lucas in town

I heard my voice. I saw the soft skin of my hands. He pressed himself against my chest, put his mouth on me, found a way to suck in the sound of my heart. "Come," I said to Clara one afternoon, as I held him, as she watched us, saw me, mother. "Come here, Clarita." She came. I pulled her close. We stood together, the dyad now a triad, three points, the triangle nature's strongest shape.

A year after Lucas's birth, Ceci's visa expired. In order to renew it, she needed to return to Mexico, submit an application, and wait for a response from the embassy there. Her chances of getting a new visa: fifty-fifty. My husband and I did whatever we could, sought legal aid, attempted sponsorship, suggested she marry her American boyfriend. In the end there was no choice but for her to leave us for many months, maybe forever. I cried and cried. I cried mostly for Clara, such a huge loss, so early on, and I cried for the girl I once was, standing in front of my house on a hot summer day, waving good-bye to my own mother as the car drove me far away—forever—and who knew when, if ever, we would see each other again. I cried in relief and fear, the sense of something opening, something ending. Clara cried too. That night, she slept with me, in my bed. Dreaming, she moved towards me. "We are finally finding each other," I thought.

Ceci had left behind her clothes, her shoes, her artwork, she was everywhere in our home, her plan to return obvious. But a few days after she left, I found myself packing up her clothes, slowly at first, and then picking up speed, boxing the dresses and skirts and shirts, moving her toothbrush and cosmetics into storage, taking down the puzzle pictures, the lacquer shiny, the cracks everywhere.

"What are you doing?" my daughter asked.

I knelt down, took her chin in my hand. "I know Ceci is your very best friend," I said.

She nodded.

"But she is not your actual family," I said. "Ceci has her own family, in Mexico."

"I know," she said. She looked straight at me. "I know you're my mother," she said. "And Ceci is my stepmother."

"No," I said. "Ceci is your nanny. She loves you with her whole heart. But nannies do not stay forever, even though they love you forever."

"Do mothers stay forever?" she asked.

"Most mothers do," I said. "Some don't. But this mother," and I pointed to myself, "this mother will stay with you for as long as you want."

"Until you die," she said.

"Yes," I said. "Until I die."

"When will you die?" she asked.

"I hope not for a long time."

"I know you will die before Papa," she said.

"How do you know that?" I asked.

"You're forty-one," she said. "And he's only forty."

"You never know," I said. "But don't worry."

"I'm not worried," she said. "I'm not the worrier. You are."

"You're right," I said. "I worry."

"Someday," she said, "Ceci will have her own baby."

"I hope so," I said.

"And you know what I'm going to be when I grow up?" she said.

"No," I said.

"That baby's nanny," she said. "I'm going to be Ceci's baby's nanny and a mama too."

"That's a great plan," I said.

"My plan," she said, "is to have four babies of my own, plus take care of Ceci's. So that's five," she said. "That's my limit."

We hired someone else to take Ceci's place during the months she was in Mexico. Vanessa was not nearly as good. She lacked Ceci's keen competence, her motivation, her spark and humor. She lacked the enormous blessed love Ceci had to give, and this too was, in its own way, fine with me, for I felt I had more room, more say-so, more authority and simple space. There were small tasks Ceci had always done without ever being asked, like making Clara's lunch for school each day. Now that fell to me. It is important to make your child's lunch. It is important to cut the bread, wrap it, arrange the lunchbox, tuck in a sweet snack. It is important to know that when, the next day, she opens it, she will briefly see that in the arrangement and choice of foods, you have loved her, and always will.

It is important to claim the tasks of motherhood, even when time or trauma makes it difficult. You must, of course, sign the permission slips, shop for shoes, cook when you can, do her hair, with or without the knack. How one balances this with the competing demands of career or long-standing insecurities, I really have no idea. No advice. Only that it must be done, here and there, wherever you can. Motherhood is at once a great and sentimental abstraction and, in its true nature, a series of tiny tasks, not a lifetime but a day, which brings you to another day, which brings you to a third, and so you go. It is all dirty work, full of germs and life.

I gave my mothering away, and for too long a time. I did it one-eighth out of busyness and seven-eighths out of fear. I did it because I had the great good luck and simultaneous misfortune to find another mother so willing and skillful, so comfortably maternal, that I could not quite find my way, my voice, so to speak, the silly songs, the lettuce leaves. I did it also, and paradoxically, out of a keen desire to protect my girl, my best girl, my great love, from the badness I believed was in me. My daughter, my son, I owe everything to them. They have given me more than anyone could ever ask for. They have proven, by their very ruddy and vigorous existences, that even though my own mother gave me up and found me flawed, I had at least two good eggs to give the world, and I gave them.

Ceci was, after several months, granted a new visa and wanted to return to work. But I knew it could not be. I knew I had stepped into some new space and wanted not to step back but forward, enlarging my maternal role, helped but not too much. To say we "fired" Ceci would be wrong, but we did let her go, the perfect nanny, Mary Poppins, who in the end drifts up on an umbrella, leaving the children to their parents' care. Ceci had no umbrella and the rupture was painful, her sense of betrayal enormous and understandable. "No," I told her over the phone, "no, Ceci, we love you absolutely, but we just don't need . . ."

"It is up to you," she said.

"We will find you another job," I said. "We will find you a rich family who can pay you more."

"I can take care of myself," she said.

We both hung up, in tears.

Every once in a while now Ceci visits us. She is, indeed, working for a far wealthier family, earning much better money, so all's well that ends well. Sort of. "You know," Ceci said to me a few weeks ago when she was visiting, "Vanessa is not keeping up Clara's Spanish. Since I've been gone, Clara's Spanish has really degraded."

"I will talk to Vanessa," I said.

"Clara doesn't like Vanessa," Ceci said.

"Clara will never love another nanny the way she loves you," I said.

But the strange thing is, while that is true, it is also too dramatic. For Clara, the transition was terrible, but she has moved on. When Ceci comes to visit, she spends less and less time with her, wanting to leave after only a minute now, to play with her best friend next door. So Ceci and I are left together, sitting in the kitchen, watching the girl we both love best out the window, playing on the green grass of our neighbor's yard. Upstairs, Lucas, the boy I love best, churns in his sleep, the monitor crackling, full of the sound of him. "I have always wanted to ask you," Ceci said to me one day, "why did you fire me?"

"I didn't fire you," I said, then began to stammer: "I didn't need as many hours . . . we were . . . the money . . . expensive . . . I didn't want to work so much—"

"Were you jealous?" Ceci interrupted.

Brief pause. "Yes," I said. "You were always the better mother."

"That is not so," she said. Her eyes filled with tears. "I am thirty-eight," she said. "Clara may be the closest I ever get to having my own daughter."

"She belongs to both of us," I said.

But it was clear, looking out the window, that Clara belonged to no one but herself. There she was, leaping up to catch a ball, dancing in a clown costume, holding hands with Maya, her best friend. I tapped on the window. Clara looked up, briefly waved at us, went back to the business of her life. Ceci and I sat together in the kitchen. It was so quiet. We could hear the heat turn on, the furnace tick and fire. We boiled water on the stove. We filled our mugs, peppermint and chamomile. In the end, the unbreakable bond was perhaps not between Ceci and Clara or between Clara and me, but between Ceci and me, two women, two other mothers, knowing without words how hard and fierce and fabulous mothering can be, understanding the inherent losses of it all, soothing ourselves together, here, in the kitchen, at the very end what is left: two women taking tea.

10

The Suit

I've never been good at fashion. Some people have the knack; even a scarf flung casually about their neck looks somehow silken and august. I, on the other hand, am a rumpled person, both literally and philosophically. I see the universe as messy, black cloth crumpled with pins and rips. My view is fundamentally pessimistic. I have never understood the expression "freak accident." Given the existence of black holes and burst blood vessels, it astounds me that anyone really has the courage to get dressed up in the morning. Accidents are not the exception. They are the rule. Therefore, one should outfit oneself accordingly. The truly paranoid should wear yellow hard hats and carry candles. The others, like me, who live on the perpetual edge of an overprocessed ironic worry, should just be frumpy. And that is what I am.

One of my earliest memories involves clothes. I was six years old. I had a great future in front of me. I wanted to be a zoologist, a chemist, a teacher, and a tailor. Mrs. Pichonio, the old widow who lived down the street from us and had a magnificent high hump in her bent back, owned a sewing machine. It was stored in a golden-wood cabinet with iron scrollwork legs and many miniature drawers. The machine itself had Singer written on it, each letter red and formed from tiny painted flowers. The needle nosed in, nosed out with a chattering sound. Once she let me try it, and it amazed me, that cloth could come together, that the open ended could be so easily seamed, that you could cuff and button and hem.

Back at home, I set to work with a plain old needle and thread, the only supplies I could find, plus a large swatch of pink fabric from my mother's rag basket. Within a few days I had fashioned for myself a skirt, a lopsided article of clothing, sticky with glue and snarled with knots. I proudly wore it to school. Having become frustrated with the process of fastening silver snaps, I simply clasped it at my back with masking tape. I was not the kind of kid one laughed at; people simply stared.

Thus began my clothing career, or what I should more accurately term my anti–clothing career. I looked like a frowzer, and I loved it. After a while, the love went away and it became my habit, a manifestation of who I essentially was, something snarled. I lost my interest in sewing, no surprise, but the tendency towards clothes that did not fit, ugly clothes, sloppy clothes—that became ingrained. For the past twenty or thirty years, almost every day, I have rolled out of bed, grabbed for the raveled sweater, the paint-splattered pants. I never understood why people bothered to change their outfit *every day.* I have always worn the same outfit, minus the underwear, for one week at a time. It cuts down on laundry and so simplifies things. During the darkest parts of my life, I have even slept in my clothes, thereby avoiding the tiring task of getting dressed in the morning.

That I am a writer, a freelancer with no office to go to, has only more deeply ingrained my tendency. But as occasionally happens to writers, a few weeks ago, someone read my work and liked it and asked me to go on TV for two minutes. That didn't excite me. I have been on TV for two minutes before and I've long lost the illusion it will make me famous. And it probably doesn't help that I have almost always refused the makeup, with the exception of my *Oprah* appearance, because she insisted.

The publishing company, however, the one that has consented to print my work despite obvious profit loss, that company did not share my attitude. For the publicist this was a great opportunity—it was CNN—and she instructed me to dress accordingly. She knew me. She knew that without firm direction and tutelage I would probably not look good. She told me to go to Ann Taylor and buy a suit. A suit! "Expense it to us," she said, sounding a little desperate. Ann Taylor! I only shop at Target, and before Target came to the East Coast, I shopped at Bradlees, whose bankruptcy I am still in the process of mourning.

The publicist was so insistent upon the suit, and so worried I wouldn't obey, that in the end she traveled from New York to Boston, where I live and where the filming was, in order to supervise my shopping. She wanted to go with me to Ann Taylor to pick out my clothes. This I knew I could not do. One does not show one's publicist the unpublic places, the bulges and lumps. I said I would go on my own.

Of course, I didn't. I went straight to Target and found a red suit for thirty dollars. I thought it looked fine. It didn't entirely fit, the sleeves of the jacket were too long and the skirt was a little loose, but these were minor details, and besides, they usually only film from the neck up. I liked this suit. The red made me look happy; it underscored the flush in my face. It lit up my skin.

I went home and tried it on for my husband. "You look," he said, "like you're about to go trick-or-treating."

I returned the suit. I did not want to get the publicist mad. I knew she was not after a style with any witch in it. I thought my husband was wrong, but I wasn't going to risk it.

The next day, a Sunday, I conceded. I went to Ann Taylor. The store was in a mall, and I try to avoid malls as much as possible due to potential terrorist attacks. I figured, however, it was Sunday, I was there first thing, the mall was relatively empty, it was not prime time in terms of bombs or aerosolized chemicals. I thought as soon as I stepped foot in the mall I would get sweaty, but in fact, that didn't happen. The mall was nice. It smelled of coffee and had booths selling wind chimes and wigs and glass cats. It was almost whimsical.

Ann Taylor itself had a charmed hush to it. There were a few women there, and they drifted between the racks of clothes like wraiths—angels or ghosts. I collided with cashmere. There was a white sweater and a matching white scarf, and it was as soft as snow to touch, but warm. I studied some velvet. It was satisfyingly raspy. These clothes were gorgeous; anyone could see that. They called attention not so much to themselves as to the way the light fell around their forms, suggesting the body beneath, at once sheathed and open.

A saleslady drifted up to me. I told her my situation, that I needed a suit and I needed it fast. She was so gracious. She flicked through the racks of soft things and stylish things and held them up to me with complete confidence. If I seemed strange to her in my big rubber boots with old overalls tucked in, she didn't show it, not a bit. I was another customer, her charge, her mission for the moment. She brought me back to a dressing room and handed me jackets and skirts and shirts. The clothing felt cool against my skin, and it all looked good. I am not accustomed to having clothes that truly fit. I have always been content with an approximate fit, tending towards the too large. These jackets enclosed my waist, and had whalebone buttons. The skirts were straight and slit. I was, she informed me, a petite. I thought of Hans Christian Andersen's wonderful tale "Thumbelina" and the big red flower and the river and the butterfly. Petite! In fact, I was extra petite. Size six petite didn't fit me; size four, still too large; size two, close but not quite; size zero, perfect. On the one hand, I was truly proud. For what woman would not consider size zero to be an actual accomplishment? On the other hand, a zero? It was, for sure, a mixed message.

But here's what really mattered: In the size-zero suit, I looked great. I looked serious and sexy. I looked like a lawyer, like someone in a high-rise, a woman with extra influence. The transformation was total, in part because of the fit. The suit at once concealed and revealed my shape. I had a shape! I had a little waist. I had a visible collarbone, which gave me an appropriately gaunt look. My throat was white and long.

I bought the suit, several hundred bucks, and on sale too. She gave it to me in a bag with velvet handles. She asked me if I'd like shoes to go with the outfit, but I was overcome, overwhelmed, and out of money. I told her no on the shoes. I said I already had some. Then, on my way out of the mall, I snuck into Payless, a discount shoe emporium, and got a fourteen-dollar pair of pumps.

At home, I tried on the suit in front of my full-length mirror. I was wondering whether the mirrors at Ann Taylor were rigged in some way and that now, face-to-face with the glass on the back of my closet door, I would see the truth. And I did see the truth. The truth was I still looked good: My waist was still small. My collarbone flared. I had a charming freckle on my chest.

The next morning, when I woke up, I didn't reach for the raveled sweater and paint-splattered pants. I put on the suit. It was slightly itchy but immensely gratifying. I went to work, which for me amounts to traveling from my bedroom to my study, across the hall. Usually I work in some version of my pajamas, but today was different; I decided to get all dressed up, as though to meet my characters. My writing was sharper because of that suit. My characters all said witty things, and my overwrought lyricism gave way to a kind of muscular minimalism. I started to think the suit was magic.

I went on TV the next day and I was very articulate. My publicist, who herself was wearing a suit and mauve lipstick and slingback shoes, was impressed. Huge white lights shone down on me, and behind me stood a man with a silver disc. Then it was over. I went home. The house seemed oddly quiet, in a way both creepy and peaceful. The sheer curtains billowed with sunshine. The cat wreathed around my legs. I stripped and hung the suit way in the back of my peeling closet.

But something was different. Even with the suit off, I still felt like it was a little bit on. My walk was more purposeful. I felt *aloft*. I felt pretty and I liked it. I began to wonder about Botox. I pinched my lips to plump them out and, sure enough, that made me prettier still. Suddenly, there were so many possibilities. Perhaps I should get a perm, some smart, springy, sexy curls to accompany and enhance my new image. I bought a fashion magazine and went to see a stylist at Lord's and Lady's. She grabbed a hunk of my hair and said, "Perm, no way. You're much too brittle."

"But I have hairspray on," I said, which I did, part of my new experimentation. "I have a lot of hairspray on. Without it, my hair is not so brittle."

"You don't need a perm," she said. "You need color."

Color it was. My strands stripped of their darkness and gray, saturated with something gold. My husband reacted exactly as he was
supposed to, just like a husband on a perfume commercial: "Wow,"
he said.

I could go on. And on. I could tell you about the lid lift I thought
of getting, the tarry mascara I bought, the fancy shampoo with a
lather as rich as a racehorse's. I could tell you about the pants, but I
won't. The clothes are at once entirely the point and not at all relevant. What matters is this: I began to see the surface of everything,
the shifting surfaces of people's faces, the grainy surface of my desk-
top, the surface of the sky, all slick and blue. I saw the surface of my
body and ignored the bones. And this was all very good. Not only
was it fun; it was somehow, somehow *healing*, to use a surfacy word. I
bobbed to the top of life and blew a bubble or two. I began to understand that a life dedicated to appearances was not, in fact, a shallow
life; it was life lived at the pitch of drama, life on a stage, life acted
and enacted, almost Shakespearian. When you tend to your surface,
you are making an image, and images are the essence of art. When
you tend to your surface you are making a statement of faith. You are
saying, *I matter.* You are saying, *The world is worth dressing for.* You are
engaging in the best kind of optimism, an optimism that propels you
out of bed in the morning, that directs you to the day. When you
put on nice clothes, you are putting on hope, you are saying, *Here I
am. This is fun. Look at me.* You are jerked out of your scrunched existence and into possibility: the pretty, the silky, the tweed. You are
celebrating the excellent malleability of human experience, that you
can be this and you can be that, the fusion of image with flesh.

But at the end of the day, of course, you have to take your
clothes off. Unless you want to sleep in your suit, this act of un-
dressing cannot be avoided. The night air is cold. An airplane roars.
A grandmother has just died, and as well-dressed in her coffin as
she was, she still looked, well, she still looked dead, the swoop of
blush hideous on her sallow skin.

I wonder if there are some people who never get undressed, or
who always stay well-dressed, in a metaphorical sense. If there are,
I salute them. To go through life clad and stylishly clothed, with all

the relentless optimism this implies, is in and of itself a herculean feat. I, in the end, do not have this stamina. I cannot run that race. I cannot bring myself, when all is said and done and stripped, to see the fabric of the universe as anything other than rumpled. Clothes are a grand vacation, an excellent adventure, but in the end, you come back to your body.

My body is aging. I have warts on my feet. My hair is brittle, with strands of gray beneath the saturating gold. I cannot stick to my surface. I sink, and in that downward decline, in the quiet moments, with the suit hung up in the closet, the flared velvet pants put away, in the quiet moments lying side by side with my infant son as he falls asleep, I think of frightening things. And it occurs to me, in these unclad moments when the world comes at me raw, it occurs to me that my images of terror are as commodified and commercialized as my newfound interest in clothes. I mourn what the media tells me to mourn. I now dress as the media tells me to dress. Even my deepest fears have a sort of surfacy feel to them, aerosolized toxins and jihadists in kaffiyeh.

What are the real dangers here? What are the actual risks that exist beneath the fabric of our American lives, beneath all our stylized surges? I cannot answer that question. Perhaps the answer is simple, though. Perhaps it has something to do with a grandmother in a grave, the way our faces crumple in time, our ends, however they happen. A person cannot tolerate it all; it is too much. Clothes are as fine a diversion as any. They may not remake your soul, but they give you a much-needed break. I would like a gown, pale blue, seeded with pearls at its collar and cuffs. I would like to dress my children in everything Gap. I would like us all to go forward, together, as beautifully bandaged as a human may be.

11

Bilateral

Once, when I was a child, I milked a cow and didn't like it. I remember the beast, sizzling with black flies, hair matted with dung, one cloven hoof dangling delicately in the air as I closed my fist around a teat and squeezed. Milk spurted into the bucket, a bluish-white warm liquid with something scummy on top. The beast pawed at the ground, turned her huge head, looked at me. Go *on*, she seemed to say. Her udder was hot and hard, her nipples as big as pinkies, indecent.

Years later, when my own breasts began to grow, I thought of that cow. My mammary glands turned so tender they would ache when the wind blew. Now, in my thirties, I am five feet, one hundred pounds, and my breasts, double-D cup size, have always exhausted and embarrassed me.

Therefore, it was easy for me to decide, when my most recent breast biopsy came back bad, that I wanted a mastectomy. It was a Tuesday. It was late winter, snow still gleaming on the ground, and the doctor called to tell me: *atypical ductal and lobular hyperplasia*. The lump that had been plaguing me for the past eight months turned out to be stuffed with rusty cells, misshapen and exuberant, multiplying much too fast. *Atypia* isn't cancer; it's the thing before cancer, the warning sign, the announcement before the building blows up. I asked my surgeon right there over the phone what percentage of women diagnosed with atypical hyperplasia go on to develop carcinomas, and she said no one knew. No one knew! Is this not ridiculous, blasphemous, that no one has yet done a simple study that follows, say, one thousand "atypical" women for a period of years and sees who dies, who doesn't?

That day, I made an appointment to see a surgeon, to discuss next steps. I already knew what I wanted to do. I have two close relatives who have had breast cancer; I've had a child over the age of thirty-five; I am Ashkenazi Jewish; and for the past eight years I've had to subject my enormous lumpy breasts to countless mammograms, sonograms, MRIs, and biopsies, and this well before I'd hit forty. Early-detection technology obviously saves lives, but it wrecks minds; you live in the terrible grip of waiting. I made an appointment with my surgeon, and the morning of, I went to the farm near my home to look at cows. They were waiting to be milked, kicking at their painful udders, their breath hot-sweet blasts in the winter air.

My surgeon's office is in a stark, practical building with little color. The halls are hushed, the few decorations rational. She started to tell me about all my treatment choices and I interrupted her, a slash with my hand, "I want a mastectomy," I said. "Now."

"Is that really what you want?" she asked. "We have so many advanced techniques, like the MRI, for early detection, and breast-conserving therapy, and you can take tamoxifen. . . ."

But I didn't want to discuss it. I had touched a cow and found it distasteful. I had had my babies, so whatever utilitarian purposes my two external placentas might serve were all gone anyway. More important, I didn't want the psychological torture of endless testing. Modern breast-cancer detection, while it's obviously done great good, puts women in a stark conundrum. Advanced mammography, frequent and accurate biopsies, and nifty MRIs all enable both patient and doctor to see conditions whose prognosis they do not know. The hazy, maybe prognosis, like atypical hyperplasia, that could or could not become cancer, or ductal carcinoma in situ, that might or might not spread, means you live your life on high alert, hitched to your oncologist, who checks you at the slightest

sign. No, I didn't want that. I chose the most extreme medical intervention—bilateral mastectomy—to get out of a lifetime of more
minor medical interventions with serious psychological side effects.
It's no way to live, as a screening devotee. Better to take what time
you have left and be blissfully ignorant, than to whittle it away
worried over what result, when and how.

My surgeon said, "Maybe you should think about it. There's no
emergency here. Take your time and think it through."

"I've thought it through," I said. "A) I'm not at all attached to
these breasts, and B) I can't live my life in an MRI machine."

She said, "Give it a couple of months."

I said okay, but I knew I wouldn't wait that long. I was done
with waiting.

My husband was tentative. "I really like your breasts," he said, but
he knew I didn't like them. He'd seen me lift the ledge of them up
on a hot day. He'd seen me sweat out countless biopsies too. He
said, "Without your breasts you'll look weird." I said, "With my
breasts I look weird."

I convinced my surgeon that a mastectomy was truly what I
wanted to do. In the week or so before the procedure, a kind of elation filled me. Here I was, diagnosed with a dangerous condition,
and I was high, high on the cold, clear winter air and the fashion possibilities in front of me and the freedom: no more screen-
ings, my breast-cancer risk plummeting. A mastectomied woman
can still get breast cancer, but studies show that she has only a 5 to
10 percent chance, and that's a lot lower than you. Or you. Or me,
who, with all my combined risk factors, had a whopping 90 to 100
percent lifetime chance (my surgeon finally came up with some
stats), good god. Why wouldn't I cut off my breasts? Why doesn't
everyone? I sometimes wonder this.

I visited a plastic surgeon who told me to take off my shirt.
"Well," he said, "you are large. We'll make you a B," and then he
showed me the breast that would go in me, a jellyfish-like saline-
filled sac, almost pornographically pert.

As the days drew closer, my elation turned almost manic. Dr. Poires, my surgeon, said, "I'd like you to see a therapist. A woman should grieve before she loses her breasts."

Is this true? Did I have grief I was covering up? I went home and stood naked in front of my mirror. I eyed my mammary glands for a long, long time. Through the pale skin I could see the roaming of veins, green veins, running from my throat, snarling in my chest, and fingering their way into my pale, pale breasts. I could see how the seam of the breast was connected to the chest wall, beneath which hammered the heart. When I breathed, my breasts rose up on the lobes of my lungs; breath and breast. Heart and breast. Flesh and breast. What I saw, standing there, was that the breast is an integral part of the body, its intricate ecosystem, which, when severed, would cause pain. I didn't doubt my decision then, but I had a long moment of feeling bad for my body, and bad for my breasts, which I was abandoning in cold blood, a piece of me, killed off.

I went into the surgery with my head held high, a tight scoop-necked shirt from the Gap packed into my bag, what I would wear on the way home. There was a damsel fly in the surgical waiting room, one of those leggy primitive insects, and I thought that was strange, a bug in the hospital, but I wasn't scared. I wouldn't take it as a sign.

I was shown to a cubicle, where I undressed and lay on a stretcher. The man in the cubicle across from me appeared to have no legs and only one arm. He was pretty much torso topped with brain. I couldn't stop staring at him. He saw me staring and waved.

The anesthesiologist came around. He told me his name was Dr. Drown. This is when I started to feel definitely scared, but I also thought it was funny. Dr. Drown had a teal-green surgery cap and a mask over his mouth, so I could not completely see him or assess him. Dr. Poires, the breast surgeon, came in; she looked funny in her scrubs and masked mouth, like a criminal. They wheeled me down the long hall.

Dr. Drown put me out; he flicked a neural switch and I was down, drowned, and then I bubbled up to consciousness again, nine hours later, in a room I had never seen. I knew immediately that my breasts were gone. My chest felt terrifyingly light, like it was filled with only cotton, and then there was a long, slow, curving pain that took its time with me.

I was baked on drugs, still swimming in the liquid-glass of anesthesia, but my mind was strangely, awfully clear. I could feel the sawed incisions, the enormity of the amputation, and how hard it was to breathe. "Breathe, breathe," a recovery room nurse kept yelling to me, and a machine above me was beeping out some warning, and I didn't want to breathe; I wanted just to sink, and I thought I was possibly dying, sometimes people do die from surgery, and right then and there, just after the operation, I regretted my decision.

I wanted my breasts back.

I wanted my body back: my breath, my ability to move, my blood pressure, which was something like 50 over 40, a common but problematic response to anesthesia. "*Breathe, Lauren,*" the nurses commanded, and I tried to recall what percentage of people do pass on, from complications. Did I have a complication, or was everything okay? "Am I okay, am I okay?" I kept saying, and they kept saying, "You're okay," and then the machine would beep and they'd shout, "Breathe!" so it was a mixed message.

Despite the anesthesia, I was in great pain. And right there in the recovery room, I got a bit more acquainted with death. I saw my baby girl, not as she was, a five-year-old, but as she'd been when she was born, her lids creamy and clamped closed.

Then my blood pressure stabilized enough so that they could bring me to my room. It was midnight; the surgery had started at two that afternoon. My husband was in the room, and in the dark he held my hand. I could just make out the crimson skulls of flowers, and behind them, in the glass square, flecks of stars with no names. I said to my husband, "Don't leave me here," but at some point he did, he was just too tired, and so I stayed alone, and I listened to my heart, clomping like a heavy hoof, I could hear it. Without my breasts, I was that much closer to my bones, my body.

Mastectomy is not a makeover. I was mistaken in thinking it would be. No. Mastectomy is a brutal operation where your breasts are ripped out at the roots, where you wake up in significant pain, where, when you finally see the hatchet job, you want to gag. My chest was bulldozed, like a refugee camp, a lot of blood and rubble.

I stayed in the hospital for four days. So did my breasts, the ones that had been removed, they were ten stories below me, smeared on some slide, being read for cancer. Dr. Poires told me, on my third hospital day, that the left breast had been okay but that the right was full of misshapen cells, and later, when I saw an oncologist, the oncologist said, "The line between what you had and cancer is arbitrary. Two pathologists read your slides and one saw carcinoma."

When I heard this, I was truly glad I'd removed my breasts, but I wasn't elated anymore. It is *not* a makeover, and it is *not* a guarantee. The recovery is difficult. I couldn't lift a coffee cup, or my baby, for months. I had drains inserted, and for two full weeks a zinfandel-colored pus collected in the plastic bulbs, which I had to empty every hour or so. The anesthesia, which I was under for so many, many hours, seemed to seep into my bones like radium, and that, combined with a steady dose of pain pills, made me dumb and eventually very depressed.

I write today, a little more than one year after the procedure. It has been a June of fantastic weather, river-blue skies, a profusion of roses, the scent of sheared lawn from the man and the mower next door. June is a fine month, a hammock month, and I have been doing that, lying back. I am finally feeling better now, although it's taken me a long, long time. I can lift my child with effort. I can scrub the floor, even though that hurts. I can sleep without the pain pills. And yesterday I went shopping, for the first time, buying the little shirts and Lycra I had said I so wanted, and still do, but with much, much more sobriety.

I don't know that I won't get breast cancer, or that the cancer one pathologist said I had will not return. As I said, mastectomy reduces but by no means removes the chance. What I do know, though, is that I won't be living my life in a mammography studio or an MRI machine, or waiting for billions of biopsies to come back, because, while I have some tissue, it's not even enough to biopsy, really, and it's not nearly enough for a mammogram. As for the body-image issue, I do like my body better, in clothes anyway, with my pert B-cups—but I don't want to overstate it. Implants are not pretty when you see them "in the flesh." They are obviously fake, nippleless mounds, with dark-pink shiny scars and puckers on them. Sometimes I miss my old big breasts; I wonder what became of them, if they were thrown into the trash bin at the back of the hospital, if they somehow sense my betrayal.

I say I'm sorry.

I say it to my real breasts, my true breasts, that I betrayed even as they betrayed me, and I say it to the body left behind, for it has had an intricate part of its ecosystem just carved out, and I say it to all other women who must tussle with a difficult choice between mutilation and temporary peace of mind, and I say it to my daughter—I'm sorry—because when she sees me naked now, she looks away.

This is the truth, and she's so young.

"What happened to you?" she says.

Next door to us, Corinna, our lovely neighbor, has had her second baby. Corinna's body is intact. My daughter and I go to visit the baby, and not long after, the baby starts to squall, and Corinna lifts her shirt and brings the infant to her chest. My daughter, who knows nothing of etiquette, stares at Corinna's giving nipple, she just stares and stares, at the breast, the baby, the white markings of milk on its tiny mouth.

Later on at home, my daughter turns to me. "Let's pretend I'm a baby," she says.

"Okay," I say.

"Ga ga," she says, and then she comes over and lifts my shirt.

"What are you doing?" I say, I practically shout, but she says, "I'm a baby, you have to feed me," and then, my god, she puts her mouth where my nipple once was and pretends. She just pretends. I want to cry. I hold her close. I am so sad she doesn't have me as a full-bodied woman, but I'm so glad I have a better chance of lasting until the time when her own breasts fill.

12

Zyprexa

My blood is in a blender. It's just about the only bit of brightness in this drab office of a life insurance company that, before it'll bet on my body, feels the need to sample its various fluids—specifically urine in a tiny pleated cup and, now, my blood in some sort of centrifuge the phlebotomist switches on. It circles, at first slowly, then picking up speed until it's whipping my life-source so thoroughly that, at last, the lipids separate from the fresh red liquid and rise to the top—that's cholesterol I'm seeing, a custardy yellow substance that reminds me of the pudding my mother used to make. Damn my mother! It's her cakes and tarts and tortes that have put me in this position, which is precisely . . . what? I'm a forty-seven-year-old fatso with a penchant for Belgian waffles. In truth, though, it's neither my mother nor those waffles that are responsible for my body's breakdown. Isn't this terminology odd? *Breakdown*. My body is having a breakdown, for sure, yet instead of atomizing into pieces and parts, I'm doing just the opposite. I'm acquiring a perverse sort of solidity that belies the real crux of the matter. For sure, no breeze will blow me over, but that doesn't mean I'm strong. My breakdown is a kind of hyperplasic excess that renders me easily winded and, nearly worse, has exiled me to the X section of clothing stores, where I now must buy clothes in a 1X or even 2X size. Once I was five feet (I'm still five feet) and weighed one hundred pounds. What has happened here?

"Do you think they'll insure me?" I ask the phlebotomist as we look at my spinning blood and at the lipids lining its surface.

"I see this with lots of folks," the kind phlebotomist says to me, but I'm not reassured. I am now a member—along with "lots of folks"—of the American obesity club, a club I'd do almost anything to leave, the damn badge stuck to my excess skin with an adhesive that is out of this world.

This is not a story about life insurance and how hard it is to get when your cholesterol, like mine, is 405 and your triglycerides are over 800. In fact, I got the life insurance, but that didn't change my predicament. Every night I take a palmful of pills, all of them psychotropics. Way back when, in my lean, clean twenties, I needed only one pill to keep my mind aloft, but the brain is a sneaky, needy organ and even though psychiatry denies it, the brain becomes tolerant to the chemical you drink down, more often than not necessitating what is called in certain learned circles "polypharmacy" and in less learned circles, "the cocktail." My cocktail at this point consists of Effexor, 300 mgs; Wellbutrin, 300 mgs; Vyvanse, 90 mgs; Suboxone, 4 mgs; Klonopin, 1 mg; and, last but not least, the fattening drug called Zyprexa, its zippy little name not to be confused with its stuffy side effects.

All, or almost all, psychotropics cause some weight gain, but Zyprexa is in a class by itself. It was prescribed for me last year during a horrific depression. I saw black hats roll across roads and heard everywhere I went the crying of a child I could never find. At night the darkness was intense, all consuming, like liquid coal I tried to move through.

I'd always known, at least for as long as I've had my psychology degree, that severe depression can have psychotic features, but knowing is one thing and experience so entirely something else that you are humbled, thinking you had ever understood. During the summertime season, well before I'd ever heard of Zyprexa, the depression's psychotic features worsened, in part because I could not stand the contrast between my blackness and all that beauty, everywhere around me but utterly inaccessible. From the window of the kitchen I could see my garden, full of bee balm and mint, loosestrife and arctic daisies, big wheels of white with florid amber

navels packed with pollen. My garden bloomed profusely that summer, calling to it butterflies and bees and birds with yellow vests.
And yet all this beauty seemed somehow menacing to me. The
flowers—some had the heads of serpents, others flamed in the high
heat, which caused the air to warble, as though the whole world
were wavering. If I stared at my garden long enough it would dis-
solve into thousands of Pissarro points that then lost their shapes
and dripped downward.

That was when my psychopharmacologist, alarmed at my condition, decided to add another drug to my mix. First he put me on
Abilify. It didn't do the trick. Next he prescribed Geodon, which
also failed. The third drug was Zyprexa—*Zyprexa*—that zippy little
name that put me in mind of an instrument or a scooter. I liked it
from the start.

No one knows exactly why Zyprexa increases your appetite, but
everyone agrees that it does, and does so dramatically. Of all the
atypical antipsychotics, which are often prescribed as adjuncts when
your plain old antidepressant medication poops out, Zyprexa is most
associated with weight gain, and the weight gain, in turn, causes
a whole host of other dangerous problems, like diabetes, for one.
At the time I was so desperate I could have cared less about diabetes, and my doctor's warning that I might plump up as a side effect of the drug fell on fairly deaf ears. What did it matter to me
that in every study comparing "weight gain liabilities" among the
atypical antipsychotics, Zyprexa always fared the worst, with some
patients gaining over a hundred pounds, while those on Geodon
often lost weight. I knew how bad a rap Zyprexa had; I'd seen a
friend pop those pills and go practically elephantine, but from my
point of view, just then, I would have rather been a happy elephant
than a miserable hominid. Thus, I filled my script ASAP and took
my first white pill the same night. Three pills and three days later
my depression lifted, just lifted, like a wet velvet curtain, heavy and
dripping and hauled high up, above me, so I could see the air and
my garden and my whole wide world as it once was, but no, even
better. Zyprexa seemed to add a little zest, a little zing, so the edges

of everything had a merry sparkle, and I could laugh, I did laugh, finding my children's antics delightful, loving the way my dogs danced for their food. Food. *Food.* For the first time in so many months I had my appetite back and it all looked good, or better than good; it looked downright delicious, the lasagna steaming in its pan, the hot melted cheese crisped at the outer edges and bubbling on top. I could not get enough. I had the hunger of a wolf after winter, when he's gone for months with no prey. I ate mayonnaise straight from the jar, scooping it up with my paw and aiming for my face. I was insatiable, overcome, every bite was packed with complex flavors that my tongue could somehow sense, a simple pistachio nut both fruity and salty, with the wet tang of earth in the background. I rose each morning now eager for my day, packing my children's lunches and licking the Fluffernutter off the knife's blade, the taste of sweetness and sunlight. Once the kids were gone, headed off to camp, I began my own breakfast, practically panting with excitement, I'm sad to say, but it was so. Some mornings I might make oatmeal on the stove, seasoning it with cinnamon and nutmeg and several dark drops of vanilla, which gave it such a fine scent I had to have seconds and even thirds. Although at this point I wasn't giving the appetite increase and associated weight gain much thought, focused almost solely on how *happy* I was to have my life back, I still registered it as odd, that my stomach could contain so much food.

I kept going.

There were baked apple crisps with brown-sugar topping, expensive ice creams filled with real pieces of peach, and french fries, the outsides browned, the insides white and soft. I ate it all. And then more. Like so many drugs, Zyprexa's side effects were more intense in the beginning, during which time I gained about fifty pounds before coming up for air. What happened is that I saw myself. I was walking down the street towards a glass door that reflected my image back to me, but it took me several seconds to recognize myself, to register that the woman I was seeing was really me. I'd grown so stout, my facial structure buried in slabs of fat, and I thought, *Oh my god.* I went to the gym and Stairmastered myself into a frenzy, but, oddly, the exercise didn't seem to help. By this time I'd been on Zyprexa for many months and its appetite-increasing side effects had deeply diminished, and yet I was still gaining weight. "I swear to god I'm eating less than twelve hundred calories a day," I told my psychopharmacologist, but he plainly didn't believe me. "We always eat more than we think we do," he responded. I responded by keeping a food diary, just to prove him wrong, and I did prove him wrong, although I don't think he believed in the integrity of my reportage. "The fact is," I said to him, "based on my experience, Zyprexa makes you fat whether you eat a lot or not."

Some researchers agree with me, agree with the idea that Zyprexa makes you fat not because it so expands your appetite but because it radically alters how your body metabolizes the calories it takes in. Other researchers, most, in fact, see things more simply and propose that Zyprexa makes you fat simply because while on it you eat so much more. My experience with the drug contradicts this idea. Yes, I ate a lot for the first months, but after seeing myself in the door, seeing that fat reflection, I went back to eating bunny food, sliced carrots and salted celery and diet drinks for dinner, and *still* I put on weight, the scale going up, the digital red numbers burning in their black display, even my feet widening, so I went from a size six shoe to a seven to a seven and a half.

The bottom line, however, is not how or why Zyprexa makes you fat. The bottom line is that it just does, and with the excess of adipose tissue comes a whole raft of health issues, like diabetes, heart disease, and cancer, to name a few. So many patients have become diabetic on the drug that its maker, Eli Lilly, on January 4, 2007, agreed to pay up to $500 million to settle lawsuits from plaintiffs who claimed they'd developed diabetes after taking Zyprexa. Thousands more suits are still pending.

I don't plan to sue Eli Lilly for making a drug that saved my life even as it is slowly leaching it away, because I've gone into this with my eyes wide open. I do not feel fooled or tricked. Still, the fact remains that I am taking a drug that has radically raised my triglycerides and cholesterol, and put my weight at *well over* 150 pounds. It's not Eli Lilly's fault that I am now a prime candidate for any of the diseases mentioned above. That said, I suspect I have already succumbed to type 2 diabetes. During a visit to my ob-gyn, I had some blood work done and my sugar was sky high. I haven't gone to see my general practitioner to confirm the diagnosis because, well, that would have further tangled the already thorny thicket I'm caught in.

Zyprexa, as a drug, is not just about the corporeal. It actually raises some interesting, if painful, philosophical issues. A long, long time ago, well before Zyprexa or any psychotropic had yet to hit the scene, Rene Descartes, in 1641, famously came to conceive of the body as one thing and the soul, or the mind, as another. Descartes could not prove to himself that he even had a body; he could be dreaming it up, or it could be a delusion created by a demon. The mind, however, was a whole different story. Descartes *knew* he had a mind, and thus he came to the conclusion that the mind and body were so different as to exist in practically separate realms. Dualism was born, or, to be more specific, Cartesian dualism came into being, and it ruled the roost for thousands of years until, in the latter half of the twentieth century, we all grew hip to the notion that mind and brain could not be separated and, thus, mind, like body, was matter.

Zyprexa, the experience of Zyprexa, moves one out of the twenty-first century, out of the twentieth century, and back to the time of the Enlightenment, when the mind-body split was a well-accepted trope. Zyprexa makes it clear to the patient who imbibes it that she must choose between her mind or her flesh, and by doing so she is thrust back into old-fashioned dualism, ironically propelled there by one of the most high-tech drugs we have. I, for one, for now, have chosen my mind over my body, with the result that I often feel as if I lived hunched up in my head, which has to drag this offending, unfamiliar carcass all around town, the carcass being, of course, the me I have had to disown. "Go! Go now!" my mind orders the lipidinous tyrant, but she only laughs long and hard.

So, Zyprexa has banished depression and even psychosis for so many millions, while ushering in a whole new/old way of living: divided. I could go on for some time about this (the history of dualism, its appearances in the book of Genesis and in Plato's earliest writings, the role of the pineal gland in Descartes's mind-body split), but I'd be doing so as a means of evasion. What matters in the here and now is not some philosophical construct unwittingly resurrected by Big Pharma but rather what it feels like living with the consequences of that construct. I'm killing my body to save my mind, and this is downright scary. I can practically *feel* the sugar in my blood, can practically hear the crystals clanking. I realize that I am now at significantly higher risk for a heart attack or stroke as well. I can't see what I might do about these facts except to accept them as the manifestation of my decision to do dualism, to side with my mind while sending my flesh down the river.

The main effect my newfound dualism has had on me is that I no longer see my life too far into the future. When I was trim and healthy, I silently assumed, with the advent of superior medical care combined with my level of fitness, that I would live well into my nineties. Thus, being thirty, forty, forty-five—it all still seemed young, the road ahead unfurling, the end point still in mist. I even toyed with the idea that I might be a centenarian, what with thinkers like Ray Kurzweil and Aubrey de Grey suggesting that, with a few tweaks to our telomeres, we could, we can, reverse the aging process radically, perhaps indefinitely. Years ago, the cover of *Time* showed a picture of a cyborg and the headline "Can We Live Forever?" Once I would have read the accompanying article with gusto, but now I read it as a curious and somewhat sad onlooker, as a woman who does not see herself surviving past her seventies, if she's—if I'm—lucky.

My foreshortened future has some positive aspects: I take my days more seriously; I hug my children whenever I can. In a so-far-unsuccessful effort to reverse the effects of Zyprexa, I exercise hard almost every day, with the result that my weight at last has stabilized, albeit at a very high number. Every day I step on that scale and every day it stays the same, no matter how hard I sweat. But that's just one sort of scale. In reality, my life is full of scales, what one might call *the measure of our days*, and on that scale I think I'm winning. I am tremendously grateful to have my world back, to be free of the distorting depression. I take my raft of medicines at night. I always take the Zyprexa last. It's just a plain white pill;

who would have guessed it could resurrect Descartes, in addition to treating mental illness? The other drugs I slug down fast, sometimes two or three at a time, but when it comes to the Zyprexa, I put the one pill in the center of my palm, right on my lifelines— a reminder, a reassertion, that this is the choice I've made—and then I send it down the chute, while high up in my head I look all around me. My bedroom is white, my curtains so sheer they seem to be made of mist. My child comes in and wants to sleep as a sandwich tonight; can he? He asks to be between me and his papa, for no particular reason, and I tell him, *Yes. Of course.* When we turn out the light, I hear my husband on the far side snoring, and my little boy talks in his sleep of sailboats and dolphins. With all this hubbub, I'll probably be up all night. It's all right. The crickets call. A car booms as it backfires. Somewhere the ocean surges. I lie very still, surrounded. I listen, hard, to life.

13

Shame

How is it that our children can make us feel shame? We are the ones, after all, who set the rules, give the warnings, define the lines, and yet, despite our obvious authority, the truth is that there comes a time when the tiny child wields a wand more magical and fierce than any tool her parent has.

My daughter, at twelve years of age, has a pageboy cut, a pale neck where the branching veins are visible, little-girl legs lengthening, her hips just making an appearance, two demure curves. Tonight is her school concert and she looks smashing in her scoopneck shirt and short black skirt, a uniform I could never wear, my middle-aged legs too plump for a mini, my style all blend and blur. Just as she is learning to use clothes to reveal, I, nearing fifty and heavier than I've ever been, am learning to use them to conceal.

It is time to go. My daughter grabs her clarinet case and we all pile into the car, driving down dark roads, my daughter in the backseat, fitting her instrument together, moistening the reeds that make the music. "Your hair," she says to me, "is so frizzy tonight," and I nod yes, because it's true. "And you're wearing *that?*" she says, leaning over the ledge of the backseat to view my Coldwater Creek balloon pants and my long, loose shirt, the cuffs rolled. She scans me top to bottom and then turns her eye on her father, my best beloved, who is driving the vehicle. Thank god I'm not the only one. "With your beard so long," she says to him, "you look like a lumberjack."

"I can pull over to the side of the road and shave," he says. "Or better yet, why don't I shave in the school parking lot, right out in the open?"

"*Right*," my daughter says and flops back in her seat. "Just do me a favor, you guys," she says.

"Whatever you want," my husband responds.

"Just pretend you're not my parents," she says. "Pretend we've never met."

"Clara!" I say. "Never."

"Why not?" my husband says. "I remember being twelve and feeling just the same way."

We pull into the lot. As soon as the motor stops my daughter leaps from the car and disappears into the crowd of milling parents and performers, students carrying all manner of instruments: curving French horns, bronzed trumpets with their flaring mouths, silver flutes, and slender piccolos. A bell sounds and, en masse, the crowd heads towards the lit school building, inside the corridors gleaming, the walls tiled, hung with student artwork and world maps with their broad blue rivers. We enter the concert hall, the seats ascending up a carpeted slope to the top where the spotlights are. The room dims and hushes. The stage glows; on it the students are all seated, holding their instruments aloft until the conductor waves his wand and, as one, the children begin to play. Their songs soar and dip. The music they make mimics their young bodies, nimble and supple and constantly lovely, teetering on the cusp of something bigger. My husband and I, seated in the cramped back of the hall, are in seats too small, and with each passing stanza I feel my aging body bloat, inside me, my own secret song of shame.

As my daughter edges into adolescence I realize how much I'd like my old body back, the one I had when I was twenty, or even thirty, slender and athletic, the body that could do a back bend or, better yet, that could—and would—pose naked for the Polaroid, my husband clicking away, the pictures sliding from the slot all blank and milky, slowly the image resolving into itself, and what is it that we see? A nude woman flexing a substantial bicep. The same nude woman flashing her strong and slender calf. Now, facing front, plainly posed, her neck dipping down to her chest, which sports large breasts, the skin there thin as parchment, the vinery of veins visible as they crisscross, now purple, now teal, the nipples the size of quarters, topping the two mounds off. There I was. Here I am. These pictures are hidden in a pouch that is itself hidden in my desk drawer. Lately I've had the urge to show them to my daughter, just to prove to her that, once upon a time, I could strut my stuff. And yet I won't. Show her. The photos are, in the end, evidence of the private part of the relationship between my husband and me, and revealing that would be wrong. The very fact that he holds the camera and that I am posing for him suggests that we are lovers on a romp.

As my daughter teeters into womanhood, her gaze turning sharp and critical, I find my confidence waning. I join Weight Watchers, and when that doesn't work I call Jenny Craig. The woman who answers sounds young and thin and annoyingly upbeat. "How many pounds do you want to lose?" she asks. I hadn't figured that far. "A lot," I say, thinking of my slender progeny. We go through their menu and I select my foods, which arrive on my doorstep a few days later in cartons full of freeze-dried contents, the boxes hissing when I break them open with my daughter, pulling out the packages: pancakes and syrup in a small, wrapped well; a chipotle chicken sandwich with a freeze-dried side of pickles; sliced breast of turkey, the gravy in a cold lump. I sit amidst the boxes as they sweat and steam, the food scattered on the floor around me. "I can't eat this stuff," I say. "Sure you can," my daughter says. "It looks good!"

"If it looks so good, then why don't you eat it," I grumble, feeling, suddenly, very small and young in the worst way. This happens sometimes, now that my daughter is on the cusp. We'll have an interaction and I'll lose my footing as her parent, as the adult. I'll become, for a few brief moments, her peer, sour and sullen and all the more so because I can't find my footing here.

"I'm not the fat one," my daughter now retorts and when she sees my fallen face she says, "Sorry, Mom. It's just that I really worry about you."

I miss my body and, because of my daughter, I take the steps I need to take to bring my body back, if such a thing is even possible. I know it is. I've seen nubile white-haired women: slender, sexy middle-aged women with long shiny hair and cotton tights. If I try hard enough, might I become like them? Part of me is irked by my position. At fifty, or nearing fifty, you should have the right to some pudge, I think. Should not the onus of beauty fade as you age? Should you not, at some point, be able to step free from the tyranny of *pretty*? I wonder about this. I tell myself that in certain cultures— which ones I'm not sure—weight is seen as a wonderful thing, the bigger the bottom the better; so somewhere in the world is a place where I might be feted. My arguments don't soothe me though. The bottom line? I don't like my bottom, and having a coming-of-age beauty to remind me of this doesn't make it any easier.

I eat Jenny Craig for two weeks. For two weeks I microwave my freeze-dried feed, the meats, so succulent in the package pictures, are in reality grainy and tough in their texture, the sandwich buns dust in my mouth. The pickles have a tinny aftertaste and suggest a sugary flavor iced out of them long ago. Still I persist, using tall glasses of water to wash it all down, and then each morning, just as the sun illuminates night's navy clouds, turning them, tinting them, the most delicate inner-lip pink, I rise and, in the hesitant glow of a barely born dawn, I weigh myself in the bathroom, stepping off the cold tiles and onto the scale's rubber mat. The digital numbers blink and blur as they juggle for position, finally settling down just shy of the two-hundred-pound mark. They never move, day after day, meal after freeze-dried meal, the numbers have settled into a groove and, stubborn as mules, rigid and red, a pronouncement. An announcement. I begin to get angry, setting aside my appetite and refusing even a small square of chocolate. I begin to take off even my earrings when I weigh in, and then my watch, and my small Star of David. No go. The numbers won't budge.

They flicker and jiggle and then settle down: 180, 180, 180. I'm always alone when I get the bad news. I'm stark naked, in a house emptied of all its inhabitants except, of course, myself and the cat, a long-haired domestic who wreathes around my ankles and flexes his nacreous claws on the upholstered furniture. The cat, Laylo, likes my rolls and bulges. This morning, after my weigh-in, I lay back on the bed and let the cat walk the chubby plank of my prone form, which he does before settling down on my chest, where the scars are, deep pink scars, and still deeper dents from my mastectomy ten years ago.

The cat purrs, his whole body vibrating with pleasure, and I scritch his bony skull, grateful for the loose and lovely way he drapes me, his tiny, tacky tongue occasionally licking the salt from my skin. Through our large bank of bedroom windows I watch the sky progress through its morning paces, the light turning from rose to saffron as the sun ascends, its rays like ribbons tangling in the tops of trees. The cat sleeps and so do I, and when I wake there's a feeling in me, a sense that somewhere in the house something's not quite right, but what? Lately there've been scads of break-ins in our neighborhood, so we keep our doors locked. Still, I check every one. The windows, too. The floor planks creak beneath my feet, and from the kitchen window I can see the border where our open land turns to forest, dead trees forking into the air, the evergreens disappearing into the dense darkness where, at night, the coyotes pace and cry. Upstairs, I open the door to my seven-year-old son's room, ignoring his handwritten sign: *Wrning: Club membrs onlee.* His room has five skylights cut into the ceiling, so it's ablaze, aglow, the bureau lit, the bed strewn with sun, the blankets and the pillows warm to the touch. I go to my daughter's room next, facing her closed door with a feeling of dread I can't attach to anything in particular. She has the larger room but only one skylight, so while there's sun there's also shadow, lots of it, shadows that seem to have shape, form; shadows that hunch here and there, in her corners, bending under the bed, falling like cloth across her desk, which is piled high with papers and plates of half-eaten food, on her floor more papers, haphazardly tossed, a math textbook with a broken spine flat on its back. I bend down to the book and see all sorts of equations, letters and numbers, dashes and dots and boxes, fractions and decimals and divisions, none of which I understand. I see word problems: Norma gave Sam twenty-five dimes, and Sam gave Norma sixty-five pennies, so how many nickels in total do the pair have? I'm not going to take the time to figure this problem out, even though some odd *thing* in me suggests I should. The same odd *thing* directs me to my daughter's dresser, a beautiful antique I bought for her right after she was born, the wood the hue of honey, the surface scratched here and there, initialed by people in the past. Lately my daughter's been complaining about her dresser. "Why is all our furniture *antique?*" she has been asking. "I don't want to be surrounded by stuff that's old and breaks."

Comments like this remind me that she's still a child and, like children everywhere, is drawn to the bright and the bouncy, the sleek, lacking any sense that the carved initials of a stranger suggest worlds of possibility and link you to a past you might not have even known you had. I won't buy her a new dresser; I'm suddenly sure of it as I trace the ridges and scars in the beautiful planks of the furniture's surface: "E. C." "Lyle Conant." "1906." The wood, sun struck and glowing, has almost visible layers that I feel I could lift with my fingers, peeling back this palimpsest for marks made earlier still.

And as I stand there, running my hands over the marked and beautifully marred wood of my daughter's dresser, it seems only natural that I would open her drawers, just to rifle though them, just to remove the clothes outgrown, my mission not to snoop but to smooth, to organize. I pull out a pair of 6X jeans in the bottom drawer. I lift her shirts and camisoles in the middle drawer, each one smelling of clean. Holding a blouse up to the light I can see straight through the material, the blouse suddenly wraith-like, ghostly; I put it back. In her top drawer I find her underwear stuffed in crevices and corners, her socks mismatched and full of holes, and as I'm ferreting around in there I suddenly feel, with my fingers, a cool clasp, a padded mound. I pull it out and, then, dangling before me is a bra, a very small bra, to be sure, but a bra nonetheless, with a tiny rose in the crook between the two cups.

A bra. A bra! When did she get a bra? Why did she not tell me? Isn't this the quintessential confidence between a mother and her preteen daughter, the daughter murmuring to the mother that *maybe it's time*, the pair making their way to the mall to buy the bra together, the mother helping adjust the straps, finding just the right fit? The bra my daughter has bought is soft and small. I feel, suddenly, utterly inconsequential. I feel like a pendant on a slender string, just hanging. She doesn't need me. Her independence, her growth, they are, in the end, cold curves.

Yes, I miss my body, but at least theoretically, if I were to work hard enough, I could slip into slenderness again, although it might take a semi-starvation diet to do it. But as for my breasts, there is absolutely nothing I can do to bring them back. My mastectomy was ten years ago or so, after a diagnosis of atypical ductal hyperplasia and possible ductal carcinoma in situ. I swore I'd never regret my mastectomy, in part because I was tired of all the biopsies; my breasts required, each month, it seemed, a new suspicious lump, now here, now there, some big, others tiny and hard. I wanted to live free from the shadow of fear that cancer continually cast over a life filled with living purring pealing laughing beings, a house where the walls were yellow, my bedroom painted primrose blue, my gardens—all perennials—sprouting cones of lupines in the early spring and white wheels of daisies in midsummer, the plum tree growing larger each year, its rounded purple fruit falling to the soil and leaking juice that darkened the dirt and made our soil sweet. Everything, it seemed, was sprouting in my life, including my writing career, with books and essays accepted, but how hard it was to enjoy it when my fibrous breasts were sending their threatening messages, the biopsy needle plunged down deep into the suspicious masses and drawing up samples of cells that were later stained on slides and scanned. So, when the last biopsy came back bad, I said, "Lop them off," imagining that I'd finally be able to splash into my existence, like falling from a concrete rim into a warm blue pool full of flickering fish and caressing currents. "Lop them off," I'd said, because, in fact, even without their propensity for sporting problematic lumps, I'd never much liked my mammary glands anyway; they were large, far too big for my petite frame, a strain on my back and shoulders. The surgery lasted nine hours, and as I struggled to come out of the anesthesia, I ran my hand over my bandaged flatness and felt no regret, even though, already, the pain was pounding and red. I healed over six weeks and then did, indeed, plunge into the pool of my life, with no regrets, no regrets, no regrets, until, one day, today, after finding my daughter's first bra, feeling its softness, I suddenly remembered what it was like for me long, long ago, when I too was a child on the cusp of something bigger, my own breasts beginning slowly and lovely back then, then rising up out of me, aching and hot. The day before my mastectomy, my surgeon suggested writing a good-bye letter to my breasts, and I'd laughed, in private, thinking *good riddance* was more like it.

Back in my bedroom I cry into my cupped hands. The tears snake down my face and seep between my lips, tasting of tin and salt. The tears come from a place deep down and far back within me, a little knot of grief I hadn't even known I'd had: ten years later and I am finally mourning my wrecked chest. I am mourning the fact that there's nothing I can do to bring my breasts back. I am mourning the fact that never, ever will I show my daughter what is left, post-surgery, two shapeless lumps inflated by saline bags, the lumps scarred, dented, and blind—no nipples—they are icons of a war, a fraught and high-cost victory. They are *not* icons of love or nurturance or the curve of a woman's beauty. My chest is ugly, perhaps horrific, and no amount of dieting can change that.

My daughter comes back from school early today and swings by me on her way to her bedroom. "Hello," I call out, and she says an obligatory "Hi" and then disappears down the hall. I tiptoe after her. I feel like a thief. What am I doing? Why am I stalking my child? Her door is closed. I don't knock. Instead I ease it open quietly, slowly, peering in on her unaware. She's chewing on a hank of hair and typing fast on her keyboard, her back to me. Through her thin shirt I can see the jut of her spine. I was in labor with her for forty-eight hours and finally gave birth to her in an emergency C-section. They brought her to me, with her cap of dark hair and fixed crystal-blue eyes, her open mouth searching for a nipple; a hungry baby, my breasts not yet gone, she sucked down my milk, more and more and more.

"When did you buy your bra?" I finally ask her.

With her back still to me she answers without missing a beat. "About a week ago," she says.

"Why didn't you ask me, tell me? I could have helped you out."

"Papa went with me," she says.

"Papa?" I say, aghast. "Why would you want Papa to go with you and not me?"

"I figured, you know," she says, and then swivels her seat so she's facing me. "You know," she says again, gesturing towards my chest. She knows about my mastectomy. She was young when it happened. She came to visit me in the hospital, her child's face white and frightened as she scanned my bandages, bloody, the morphine pump and needles slipped into my skin.

"Just because I lost my breasts doesn't mean I can't help you buy a bra," I say.

"Okay," she says.

I stand there in her doorframe.

"Okay," she says again, and then, after another moment has passed, she says, "You can leave now. I'm kinda busy."

So I go.

There are coyotes out here, where I live. They roam the roads and rule the woods, making it unsafe for dogs and cats. Our cat, Laylo, is one tough nut, but one night, late, I hear a high, horrid scream coming from the forest, and in the morning, when I go outside, I find the corpse of our feline at the edge of a copse of trees. He is torn and opened, his fur matted with blood, his body stiff in rigor mortis. I cry into his fur, which is still, oddly, warm and then carry him back to the house and lay him on a towel. It's Sunday, so everyone is home. We all gather around the cat. "Let's all say something we loved about Laylo before we bury him," my daughter suggests. "I love how he purred," my seven-year-old son offers. "I loved how he was a night warrior," my husband says. "I loved how acrobatic he was," my daughter adds. "I loved his smarts," I say, but I'm thinking of those mornings, lying back naked on the bed, the cat atop me, luxuriating in my warmth, sharing with me his rich, reverberating purr and his dramatic glossy coat, lending me his loveliness for minutes at a time. Now I stroke the coat again, still weeping.

Later that day, despite the fact that it's Sunday, my husband leaves for his office, bringing my son along with him. Now it's just my daughter and me at home. "We need to bury Laylo," I say and she nods, but neither of us moves. We watch the cat lying, still, on the towel on the counter. When we lean close to him our breath animates his whiskers, making it seem like he's still alive. We stroke his cream-colored belly, his white socks. We kiss his small skull. Together we are tending him. We are joined by mourning, and I realize my shame is gone. So too is her ever-critical eye, filled now with falling tears. A tether between us. It's time.

We carry the cat outside. Early autumn, the trees plumes of plump color—saffron, wine, plum, crimson. The air is summer-soft but the breeze has a bite, and the hairs on my arms rise up in response. We find a suitable spot, under the stand of pines that front our country house, a place Laylo liked to lie, his bed of sun-warmed pine needles gone golden on the ground. My daughter is holding the shovel and now she raises it over her shoulder and strikes at the ground but doesn't make a dent. "Let me," I say, suddenly sure and confident. True, I am nearing fifty. True, my curves have turned to lard, my breasts to medical waste. True, I miss my old self, and this missing is made more acute by my daughter's slow acquisition of everything I've lost. But standing outside in the early fall, I realize that everything I've lost has left me with a gritty strength, with capacities I cannot even begin to calculate. My hands are lined and cracked from all the gardens I've grown, all the flowers I've coaxed up from the dark dirt. The lines around my eyes suggest everything I've seen and—oh!—I've seen a lot, so much more than she. Now I take the shovel from her and, expertly, drive it into the earth, again and again, cutting into the soil until a square grave emerges, my daughter watching, impressed, the grave neat and firm and deep down there. I lower the cat with confidence and sadness; this is something I know how to do. Nearing fifty, I've buried my fair share of felines, canines, canaries, hamsters, and even people, whom I have loved and lost. I lay Laylo in his grave-bed and then, standing, I shovel soil over him until, layer by layer, piece by piece, his body disappears and all we have of him now is a mound.

My daughter and I place a rock to mark the mound while, in the woods—it is getting towards night now—the coyotes start to sing. "I don't like it out here in the dark," she says, looking back towards the house, its windows aglow with apricot-colored light. I put my arm around my daughter. She presses herself against me. Soon, soon, we will enter the home I've made for her, but for now, out here, my body becomes her shelter as I pull her into my plush-ness and give succor.

14

Sex: In Three Positions

I.

Of all the things to write about! My sex life! My innermost inner-most. My early experience; my later affair; my typical-white-woman AIDS scare; my first orgasm with a partner, how it surprised me, how the sensation just slipped over me and suddenly I was rippling. How afterwards I hated that man (that boy, really; we could not have been much more than eighteen); I turned my face away. The intimacy was too much, too wrenching, too sizzling, shameful crumpled cry-ing coming Lauren. We were lying in his room in a boarding house, the boy just recently thrown out of a college in a far-away state for a spectacular and hard-to-achieve row of *F*'s on his report card, which he showed me—*FFFFFF*—and I could not help but think the *F*'s stood not for *failure* but for *fuck*, because he was waiting on me, I, eighteen, maybe nineteen, and still a virgin. Shame on me. Espe-cially because we'd gone out all summer before the start of our fresh-man years, his in the Midwest, mine in Boston, writing letters back and forth once September started. Not once did he ask me for inter-course, even on our last night together, but I could hear him waiting, all wrapped up in the clothing of a question: *When? When?* The very lack of his question only underscored its implicit presence.

I remember confiding to my roommate that we had not yet done the deed, even though we'd spent all summer together. Hers was a pause of shock. "You haven't gone past third?" she said. We were teenagers! And this is how teenagers talked back in the Reagan days, when you said no to drugs and yes to sex, back before AIDS, when (and probably still now) girls tossed their cherries out car windows or dropped them in the dirt like they were nothing, those fruits, that single stretch of skin. *Snap.* I didn't want to snap. *Bright blood on a white sheet.* I didn't want to bleed. Sheer fear of that plunging pain is what held me back; I couldn't insert a tampon, never mind imagine a member, its pale, smooth head with that single squinting eye, accusing, asking, pushing. *FFFFFFFFFF.* Instead of telling him the truth—that I was a mere maiden, pure as snow or cool milk in a cup—I made an elaborate lie. *I was raped. Too traumatized. I needed time.* Writing this now, remembering this now, for the first time in a long time, I do not judge myself. I consider it a lot to ask of a newly minted woman that she offer up her intact body for this frankly difficult deed. I also find it interesting that shame, an emotion supposedly lying deep in our limbic system, untouched by time or class, is in fact a product of time, and of class and culture, too. In the nineteenth century, to be raped was to be shamed, forever. In the late twentieth century, to be a virgin was to be shamed, while to be raped was to be saved, because you'd survived. After all, we not only venerate survivors; we even make them famous. But I wasn't after fame; I wanted only to escape the shame. So I lied, to save my skin. And then, during Christmas vacation, the boy brought home from the Midwest six deep, dark capital *FFFFFF*'s along with a letter from the dean saying don't come back here. Flunked out. Which is why my first orgasm happened in this rooming house in Wellesley, a mile or so from where his parents would no longer let him live. Outside, by the curb, was his slicker-yellow taxi, inside the dingy room a warming plate, a two-slot toaster, a bed with squealing springs. He was a moody, broody bad boy with a muscular chest and head roiling with glossy curls. He did downers and uppers and acid, none of which I did, but we both loved the Grateful Dead, and when I slept over (sex, but no score), we'd wake in the mornings and listen to "Ripple," the clearness of that music, the pure simplicity of it, affirming for me again and again that I was part of a people, a species, capable of creating great beauty. Such a song it was! And it was May. And the man in the room next door drank his life away. *Ripple in clear wa-ha-ter.* And through the open window, warm liquid breezes poured over our naked bodies, and then one time he touched me just so and I tipped into the orgasm and was grasped. This was different from whatever I'd achieved on my own. This was softer, gentler, full of a wide-open love, a deep falling-down love. Which is why, when it was over, I hated him. And turned my face away.

And that's all I'm going to say. I'm going to stop right here. I have discovered, in the writing of these prior paragraphs, that, while I am no longer a maiden, I am still a lady. And this is a discovery I don't know what to do with. It seems impossible, and yet, 'tis true. I find this, this assignment . . . burdensome, if not in bad taste. Am I alone in my response? Or do many women have little ladies inside? Surely I am not the only one. But it feels especially ironic that I, the teller-all of tell-alls, the four-memoir madam, should have such a teacup attitude when it comes to a task like the one I am presently engaged in. You would never guess the presence of this teacup by looking at me. From a pure looks perspective, I am as far from a lady as a mule is from a mare. Today I am wearing gray sweats, my pockets full of stones. Right this minute, as I sit here typing, I am literally weighed down by dozens of stones crammed in the capacious pockets of my tattered sweats. The stones I found this morning in a streambed by our house.

For the past three weeks, I have spent most of my mornings in this streambed, with a shovel, occasionally on my hands and knees, scraping madly to expose the pearly surface of a solid piece of past. Stones. Where did they come from? Is it possible they landed here by way of an asteroid that broke free from its planet billions of years ago, so I am finding not only stone but space? Is it possible we will someday run out of stones just as we are running out of oil, or trees? Could we survive without stones? Would we miss them, and in missing them, retrospectively discover their value? After all, think of what you can do with stones. I could build a house, a hearth, a road, a fire. Some stones you can crack open and discover, inside of them, a perfect crystallized geode. Stones are secret. Stones whisper.

I am a little lady who is also a stoner, the second part of this statement cancelling out the first. Late at night, when I am through with everything else, I boil my stones, just to see what will happen. I polish my stones with olive oil, just to see what subtle shifts in shading I might get. Today was incredible. I discovered that I could use my stained-glass grinder wheel to actually *sculpt* a stone. The stone's strength was no match for the bite of the diamond bit. I held the stone to the wet bit and felt it give way, felt it melt in my palms gone slick with stone silt as the wheel spun in water and the solid, stolid rock acquired waist and curve, acquired an impossible smoothness. When I was finished, I had a small body in my hands. This was a speckled stone body, at once utterly impenetrable and yet totally yielding. This was my body. This was my orgasm. This was my shame, my turning away, my turning to stone, my no-speak. This was my lady, here, so shapely and pursed. This was my wildness, my insanity, my boundary-breaking body and multi-memoir madam, hands slick with stone silt and yipping with glee as I discovered all I could do, one Monday in November, in my forty-fourth year around the sun, which sets so early now.

II.

I could chalk it up to age, the fact that sex interests me these days about as much as playing checkers. After all, at the unripe age of forty-four, my estrogen is probably plunging, and my periods, although still regular, are brief and bright, more like a wink than a flow.

But the fact is, I've never much liked sex, even though it has, on occasion, captivated me. I see no inconsistency here, because in general I associate captivity with guns and danger. So, yes, I have been gripped by sex the same as the trap grips the ferret's leg and he has to bite off his limb to set himself free. What kind of fun is this? Says the proverbial therapist: *Sex threatens you, Lauren. You feel overcome.*

Another definite, though altogether less *sexy*, possibility rather than feeling overcome is that I have never much liked sex because, when all's said and done, there's not much to like. I mean, really: what is the big deal? The stretch and snap and blood on the sheet is a big deal, but after that? Especially when it's with the same person, over and over again; that just couldn't be right, from an evolutionary standpoint. I, for one, have always become bored with sex within the first six months of meeting a man, assuming the man is not psychologically torturing me. Leaving those unfortunate instances aside, the fact is that sex has always paled for me just like the sun is paling these November days, and as predictably, too.

I met and fell in love with my husband for his grand good looks, his beautifully colored hair, his gentle ways, his humor, etc. We were together many years before we married and, so, sex faded. Then we decided to get married. Predictably, almost as soon as the engagement ring slid onto my finger, I fell in love with someone else. I fell madly, insanely, obsessively in love with a conservative Christian man who believed that I, as a Jew, was going to hell. We fought long and hard about that, and then had sex. This is so stupid it pains me to write about it. This man . . . he played golf. He went to church on Sundays. He wore shirts with those nasty little alligators on them. What are those shirts called—Lamaze? Or is that the name of a childbirth technique? This was not a man who cared one whit for birth-control techniques; he wanted his women barefoot and pregnant, and I fucking FELL IN LOVE WITH HIM.

I made him a beautiful chest. I worked on it for weeks. I painted the under layer white, over which I sponged a deep marine turquoise. I then shellacked twenty times, so the wood looked wrapped in glass. I painted the inside of the chest a Chinese red and decoupaged it with cut-up phrases from the New Testament. I snipped a huge and beautiful Jesus from a religious book, and then I cut the Jesus in half. I put Jesus's top half on the top half of the inside lid, his bottom half on the bottom half of the inside lid. I then shellacked Jesus until he too turned to glass. I gave my lover the box. "Open it up," I said. It was Christmastime. He did. What a spectacular gift. When you opened the lid, you saw Jesus slowly rise, resurrected, until, when the lid was raised completely, he stood solid and tall. It was a gorgeous gift that reflected a gorgeous sex life in the midst of a crazy relationship filled with clashing values and shredded bits of Bible.

And, of course, I was engaged during this whole time. A terrible thing, I know. And yet, this affair I sensed was absolutely necessary in order for me to move forward with my marriage. The affair was a test. Sex had somewhat cooled between my husband-to-be and me. I thought, but could not be sure, that that was to be my fate no matter what, no matter who, in which case my fiancé was the man I wanted to marry. But suppose I was wrong? Suppose there was someone out there with whom I could have passionate, slick sex my whole long life, a sex life like one endless Christmas morning? Wouldn't that be wonderful, especially because I'd never celebrated Christmas, so it had all the more magic and mystery to me. Thus, I fell wildly, passionately in love with a conservative Christian, very smart, very handsome, very short-sighted, and we had fantastic, obsessive sex while, the whole time, I had one eye on the clock. I was just waiting to see when, or *if*, this affair would run out of fuel. I prayed to Jesus and anyone else who might be up there that it would, so I could marry the man I loved. And yet night after night I left the man I loved to be with the man I was *in* love with. I could not wait, I was like one of those primates, what are they, bonobos, with the scarlet vaginas—yuck.

Actually, I just recalled a small detail. I don't know if it makes a difference or not. I never actually had intercourse with this man. He did not believe in sex before marriage. Therefore, when my fiancé asked me if I was "having sex" with someone else (why was I coming home at 3 a.m.?), I could answer no. On the Christian man's end, when his god asked him if he was having sex with someone else, he too could answer no, and so we both lived highly honest, righteous lives filled with perpetual sex.

But because I am not a bonobo, the inevitable started to happen. It happened the night the man took me to church and asked me to eat Jesus. Enough is enough! I am a lady, am I not? Ladies do not eat deities, and they also do not understand complicated, nonsensical theories like transubstantiation, which allows you to at once eat but not eat the deity or its stand-in, a saltine. Enough is enough and was enough. I never have and never will put the godhead in my mouth. As for the mere mortal, as for the man, after that request and all those gospel songs, after, I'd say, the twenty-third or fifty-fifth nasty little reptile appeared on his stiffly ironed shirts, he lost his appeal. Sex turned tepid, and then revolting. While the revolting part was particular to this crazy relationship, the tepid part was wholly within my experience and proved, for me, that there is no god of monogamous passion. It ain't gonna happen. Thus, freed from the tethers of this Christian affair, I returned to the gentle arms of my pagan husband, who, on occasion, also calls himself a druid. We are going on our tenth anniversary, and despite the fact that, like all good druids, he dances amongst trees real and imagined, things are tough in our fairy land. He wants hot sex. I turned tepid long, long ago.

There are treatments for this sort of thing. A 1999 University of Chicago study found that about 40 percent of all women have some sort of sexual dysfunction, usually low libido.

The real issue for me is that I'm not sure I have a dysfunction. On the one hand, I am miserable about our lack of a sex life. I am miserable about the fact that sex interests me about as much as checkers. I am miserable about it because it makes my husband miserable and cold and withdrawn, and it is so unhappy living this way. "Have sex with someone else," I tell him, and then look down at my open hands. My palms are still pinkish, but they are cracked from wear and weather. "The problem with that," my husband says, "is falling in love. If you have sex with someone else, you just might fall in love with them."

"I'd fucking kill you," I'd say.

Of course I wouldn't. But I just might kill myself.

I have no answers for how one lives without a sex drive, or with a sex drive that is equal to one's passion for checkers. The rift it creates is terribly painful, and a gulf of loneliness enters the marriage. You could fake, but fake rhymes with hate. You could get treatment, but I've had so *much* treatment, I take so *many* pills, and in this one area, just in this one small area of my life, can I claim, if not health, then at least the absence of pathology? Please? Because when I say I don't have an interest in sex, that might be a misstatement. Maybe I *do* have an interest in sex. But it's just that, comparatively speaking, I have so many other competing and stronger interests, and these interests are crammed into a life that is already overloaded. A life I nevertheless love love love love love love love love love love love love love love love love love. There are so many things I love.

Once I get past the daily dread that accompanies waking up each morning and that I cannot seem to shake no matter how blissful my state the night before, once I move past that and manage to throw my feet over the edge of the bed, then I am off, launched, singing through space, captivated by the thousands of solar systems I see everywhere. I see stones and stars. I see glass, which I cut and solder, silver liquid lines bringing scraps together in purposeful patterns. I love my wheeled mosaic nippers, how they take tiny bites out of solid opalescent or cats' paw prints and how these pieces assemble into quilts of glass, into table tops, into garden balls of deep cobalt blue. I love my garden; I love finding wild echinacea, coneflower, black-eyed Susan, even loosestrife, finding these flowers in fields or growing between bricks and then pulling them up as gently as I can and bringing them back to where I live, nursing them along, hoping through the cold winters that they will pull their perennial magic and reappear again. And half the time they do! They do! I love seed catalogues, especially in the winter, when the pictures of the glowing globes of red-hot tomatoes remind you to have faith in warmer weather. I love horses and riding them. I love my dogs, of course, and my children I love so much it hurts; they pull on me painfully, and I love them. I have recently acquired a love of stones and am making a new floor for our bathroom entirely out of pebbles the streambed has polished. I love my router, my planer, my circular saw, the wood, especially salvaged wood I can pull off of old rotting barns and restore until it's gleaming. I love clay. I like to sew and cook. I love words and writing, although that love is complex and fraught, a tense, toothy love that has made its marks on me forever.

I spent a significant portion of my life battling with significant mental illness, and my Grim Reaper, which is not death but mental illness, still visits me from time to time, drawing me down with his sword. And each time this happens I never know if I will return to love. And each time that I do, I am more grateful than the time before, and so I see my life, my large unwieldy disorganized life, as though it was a banquet full of peach and blueberry cobblers stewing in their juices, all these antioxidants, all this flesh and mineral, so much! So rich!

In our living room hangs a huge canvas sign that I, of course, made. It spells out my simple mandate, all in buttons. *Make Things*, my sign says. This is the mandate by which I live my life. As a Homo sapiens, the discovery of tools is embedded in my DNA as deeply, more deeply, perhaps, than anything else. I am quite sure that I am related to whatever ape first discovered that he or she could catch ants with a stick—oh, glory be! *Make Things*, my sign says, hung up there where my children can see, the buttons vintage and collected over many years. My sign does not say *Make Love*. I wish it did, as love is so much nicer to make, at least in sound, than *things*. But I am a person captivated by things, by solid, actual, concrete things that can be assembled, be they books or babies. Sex just does not equal or even come close to the thrill of scoring gorgeous glass for a window you will use, hearing the grit as the grains separate and the cut comes clean and perfect. Sex cannot compete with the massive yet slender body of granite I excavated out of the ground last week, six feet long this igneous stone, packed with time and stories if only it could speak. My stone. I'm going to spend months carving it with a silver chisel. I am going to figure out a way to make this stone into an enormous mantel under which, in the home I share with my husband and the babies we made, our fire will flicker. The stone will give off waves of warmth in the winter, and it will keep the night-coolness captive all through the summer days. I imagine and imagine my mantel, my windows, my glass, my gardens. I cannot believe how lucky I am. I have so very much to do, such wide and persistent passions, so little time in which to explore their many nooks and curves. Here. Now here. Don't bother me. I'm busy.

III.

And then there is the issue of sounds.

People make sounds during sex, or they try not to, if children or guests are near. The sounds you make in sex are deeply private, as are the expressions on your face, how you clench your fists, or feet, how you seize and separate. In sex—good sex, bad sex, consensual sex, or rape—you are split open and looked at. You are viewer and viewed. I find it extremely odd that on a Tuesday night you might go about this bizarre bodily act with another human being and then, the next morning, amidst a chattering group of children, eat Cheerios. It seems to me that if sex were separated out from the daily wheel of life, it might survive monogamy more intact.

For these reasons, I think deeply religious groups like the Hasidim might be on to something, whether they know it or not. I think I could be more sexual if I had a mikveh, a sacred space into which no men were allowed. In our culture, sex has lost its sacred quality. There is no withholding, no separation, no ache. I would opt for a prohibition or two—no touching allowed until Tuesday—because longing springs from distance. It is odd, ironic, but also absolutely understandable that proximity can kill sex. Devout Muslims are not even allowed to touch one another until marriage. Ooh la la. Imagine that. Imagine the long courtship in which every gesture is watched, just to be sure that not even the slightest flick of a finger lands on your lover's skin. Imagine the buildup of tension as time passes, as the wedding day draws near, as the woman is sheathed and wrapped for the pure and only purpose of being later unwrapped, after months of imagining. I know it hardly ever happens this way. But maybe sometimes it does.

The sexiest story I ever read was about a couple who never had sex. It was in a book of erotica I have recently looked for but could not find. My retelling of the story will fall flat on its face, so I'd rather not try. Suffice it to say that each day the couple, a giant and a fairy, came just millimeters closer to consummation, always leaving the bed unfinished, their days gone heavy with a ripe ache.

I have tried to tell my husband about this story, this extended extreme foreplay; he does not seem to understand. This is a problem, a classic problem that falls along gender lines. If I were mayor or president, I think I would institute some rules, some sanctions, for the good of the American Marriage.

But even with all the right rules and sanctions, we still come back to the issue of sound. Stones don't make sounds, which is maybe why I love them. They suggest sound but never utter any. And then there are the sounds of sex, which are deeply private, and which, once made in the presence of a person, can never be unmade. In the right situation, with the right sanctions, these nighttime sounds would be preserved, bottled, so they did not wash away with the laundry, the toothpaste foaming down the drain, the nine-at-night-home-from-work nights, you angry, me angry, because . . . Because.

"If you want sex," I say to my husband, "you need to have time. Sex is dependent upon time. You can't expect me to spread my legs for a man I never see, a man who is so immersed in his work he talks computer code in his sleep."

I mean what I am saying, but I also mean what I am *not* saying, and never have said, because it is too sad to say it. The sounds of sex are a shared secret between lovers, part of the glue that binds the couple together. They are considered, perhaps, the most private sounds we will ever utter in any relationship, trumping language so completely that words themselves are squashed beneath the primitive weight of the sound of sex. We have our regular speaking voices, and then we have our sexual voices, and while these voices may be odd, disturbing, even disorienting, especially if overheard by someone outside the dyad, they serve a special purpose. It is weird to me that I can have a best best friend, a friend I feel I know so completely, inside and out, but if I've never slept with her, then I don't know her sound. I need not be my best friend's lover to know her smell, her touch, how her fingers feel when they lightly land on my shoulder, but there is, locked away from me, a continent of her soul, and that is her sound.

Sounds have a powerful impact on me and always have. One of the most entrenched and disturbing memories of my childhood is of hearing my brother getting beaten by my mother. My mother beating her children, while not commonplace, was also not entirely out of the ordinary, so I was familiar with her fists, familiar with *seeing* her violence, directed mostly towards me. But there was one day when she directed herself towards my younger brother, and I did not see it. I heard it. I heard the sound of her punch, the soft, revolting smack it made in his little-boy belly, the swooshing sound of his breath, in-sucked, and then the little grunts of pain and she came down on him. Those little intermittent grunts, those disembodied cries of his, made the fact of his body all the more real, and I don't know why. I couldn't see a thing but god, good god, I could *hear* my brother's body; his flesh had entered my ear and lodged itself there, a song that can't be unsung, an insane, repetitive ditty that still today makes me gasp with horror.

The sounds of sex draw me close to my husband, when he allows himself to have them—what he says, what he does not say. But I have learned, the hard way, that while the sounds of sex are private, they are not in fact the *most* private sounds a human being is capable of uttering. I have heard sounds, from my husband, that have taken me an octave below sex, straight into annihilation, and these are sounds, like the beating of my brother, that I cannot forget, and that haunt me, and that have showed me that more private than the spasm of sex is the spasm of death. And once you have heard another human being make death sounds, you have gone too deeply down and will forever feel haunted in this person's presence.

I would prefer not to linger very long in this space of fire. It happened a long time ago, a decade ago perhaps, and late at night, midnight, I remember in fact, for the church bells had just gone off, striking twelve resonant peals that echoed in the spring air. I've told this story before, but as I retell it now, it's somehow changed.

We had married. I was finished with my affair, committed to the course ahead. My husband, who has always had a long-standing interest in chemistry, was downstairs in the basement, in a room we had built just for him, a study of sorts, lined with bookshelves upon which there were no books but bottles, and bottles, and bottles, mostly glass, some tin, all full of chemical concoctions tightly corked. His desk held Bunsen burners and glass pipettes, and a huge exhaust fan overhung the whole show, sucking out the toxic air.

And I was upstairs in the kitchen washing pots, and he was downstairs finishing some experiment—I knew not what—when all of a sudden I heard, from deep in the bowels of our house, this, this . . . *sound*, this ugly, twisted, inhumanely human, stripped, screaming sound I had never heard before but recognized immediately as pure primal terror, the sound a man makes and has made for the millions of years he's been on this planet, his body trapped in the jaws of a giant beast that is shredding him to bits. *The Sound.* I remember thinking that someone had climbed through the basement window and was murdering my husband—what else could account for that sound, as we lived no longer on the Pleistocene plains and our beasts were mostly men now.

I remember running, running as fast, so fast, as fast as I could, which was not fast enough, down the interminably long (twelve) steps to our basement floor and running across the miles of concrete (ten feet?) between the landing and the closed door to his study, behind which the screams were coming, and coming, and coming, each one rawer than the next, only "screams" in the plural is not right, because this was one solid, unrelenting scream that comes from a place deep, deep down in a person and that we usually only make in dreams we can't recall, or at the final threshold, so far gone into the darkness or light that no person can hear us, and our echo is gathered by angels or nothing.

And here I now stood, at the door that separated me from the scream. I flung it open and saw him, saw what had happened to him, my man, my lover, my husband: he had caught on fire. A spontaneous chemical combustion. His long, lovely red hair had turned to a pure rivulet of flame, and he stood there engulfed and simply screaming. I saw his hair turn to writhing snakes of fire, and then I saw the fire clasp his entire perimeter, so he stood in the center, his margins fringed with angry flames, his mouth untouched and open and the singular solid deeply private scream a man makes when faced with eternity—coming and coming and coming.

And I thought: *Five seconds ago I was a woman who had a certain story about falling in love with a red-haired man, sidestepping into a stupid, embarrassing brief affair that freed me to marry the man I loved, and now the man I love is burning up in a fire right in front of my eyes. And forever and ever this will be my story. I will be, forever and ever, a woman who watched her lover burn to death in a fire.*

This is not an essay about how my husband caught on fire. No, this is a story about sex. And sound. And stones. And snap. Don't look for the links between each position, because there may not be any, because sex is real; it is not art. It is shape-shifting and discontinuous. It has no beginning or end. Orgasms have beginnings and ends; affairs have beginnings and ends; marriages have beginnings and ends. But sex goes on and on and on for as long as this turquoise planet spins in its spot, in its particular, magical, miraculous, perfect distance from this sustaining star: our sun.

Sex is private, and the little lady in me, with her teacup on a shelf, suggests it may not be in good taste to write too, too much about it. Nevertheless, because I also have stones in the pockets of my pants, I have kicked through the lady's Do Not Enter sign and entered this essay here, only to find that though sex is indeed private, more private still is death, and that if you think you've seen your lover naked, if you think you've heard him sing his deepest self, you haven't unless, god forbid, you have witnessed what he looks like in the maw of a beast so much bigger than he. And once you have seen that, once you have heard his sounds, once you know the body of your lover as it burns away, your sex will forever be infused with fear, and rage, and smell, and echo, and you will want to push that away while, at the same time, you will want to cling all the more tightly to this friable, tender, vulnerable body of his, and yours, and yours, and yours and yours and yours and yours and yours and yours and yours and yours and yours and yours and yours. And you will come to realize that there are so many *yourses*, so many bodies, and that they are all on fire or about to be, and so sometimes it seems that the entire world is his singular scream and the terrible dangle between the stuck lever and the ejaculated mist of white.

The result of which is this: me, sitting here, pockets full of silent stones. I am a woman in love, but I am not in love with sex. I am in love with the opposite of the sound of the scream. I am in love with glass and sand and skin. I am in love with my children, my animals, my bodies, my banquet. I am in love with making but not the reverse, making (minus the *with*) love. Someday, I hope to build not only a hearth, but a house. And inside this house I want to have with me my family—my children and my animals and my husband, whom I love so imperfectly, with so many gaps and hesitations. I hope he does not leave me for a woman who likes to make love, as opposed to a woman who loves to make . . . what? What is it I love to make? Oh, I've told you that already, and besides, the list is always changing. Here I sit, pocketful of stones. Remember a long time ago, those mornings in the room in the rooming house of the boy with all his *F*'s? Remember "Ripple"? I am in love with grateful, but I am not in love with dead. The music washes over us. The orgasm is over. I remember this.

I'm at the end now. Not *my* end or *his* end, thank god. *The* end. The naked too-much truth, right here. My husband will not forgive me for my words when he reads them later on and hurt creases his whole face. *I'm sorry. I am so, so very sorry. I love you, you know. With my whole heart. You and only you.* But it is not enough. This will all come later. Right now, he hasn't seen this yet. A little bit of peace? Some unusual serenity? Sun falls across my hands, hovering over the keyboard. Nothing more can come. The computer whirs and hums; it has so many memories. So do I. And the sun falls across my hands. Everything is quiet now, except the echoes: on and on and on.

15

Tongue and Groove

We needed a new kitchen table. My husband hated the kitchen table we currently had. It was one of those islands on wheels, high off the ground, a sort of snack bar with two tall chairs that toppled easily, if you leaned the wrong way. Our daughter had leaned the wrong way a time or two, keeling to the ground like a ship filled with wind, only the landing here was hard and made of maple.

I liked our kitchen table because it had storage space. It had a drawer into which I slid my bills, usually unopened, where they remained out of sight and out of mind until the mysterious automated phone messages arrived: "This is an important call for Lauren Slater. Please return the call and cite reference number 5670890325619." At that point I would open the table's drawer and pull out my wayward bills, sticky from food that had slid in. I have always liked paying my bills in a state as stained as possible. I like to envision the recipient on the other end opening up the envelope and pulling out a check and an old french fry and feeling . . . what? Sorry for me? Guilty for harassing an overworked mother? All of my tax bills have always carried on them the contents of my kitchen table.

If it is possible for a table to be two-faced, ours was. It was a piece of furniture whose explicit mission was to provide a surface for dining, but whose implicit purpose was to allow an escape from the very domestic burdens it seemed to support. Phone bills, raveled ribbons, single socks, unsigned report cards, life insurance quotes: the table took it all in. A few times, when I'd become especially agitated at the chaos of my life, I'd picture opening the front door and sending the table sailing—swoosh—out over the porch and down the hill we lived on; there it goes. I can see it now. It careens crazily, bonking into cars, getting sucked up by its own speed, smaller and smaller it keeps going, a table with legs, it can run, it goes on and on, and then I'd picture the table swerving off the street and into some fairytale forest, where it would finally come to rest with a soft crash against the sapped trunk of a tree. And there it would live, on an enchanted carpet of pine needles, beneath a fairy-blue sky, in blessed silence and happily ever after.

If I sound disgruntled by domesticity, it's because I am. I feel, as a forty-two-year-old woman in 2006, almost obligated to say that, while simultaneously knowing that such complaints are stale and smack of other eras. Nevertheless, let me recount the whats: I dislike the dishwasher; I dislike anything having to do with diapers; I dislike car rides with my kids, those cumbersome car seats, the big jammed buckles, the straps always twisted, you bending into the backseat while the winter wind snaps at your exposed legs. I dislike shopping for birthday presents, which I think should be outlawed, all those presents, all those parties, the grown-ups milling aimlessly about, the kids with plastic forks. I dislike the flowers on the birthday cakes, big beveled roses, the sugar so dense you can taste the grit in your teeth, the rickrack of frosting that fringes the cake, which is sometimes green inside. I dislike emptying the trash; I dislike the supermarket, where red wheels of beef are sealed in plastic and pale chicken flesh bleeds pink around its edges.

But there's another side of the story to tell. I am also delighted by domesticity. For every piece of it I hate, there is a corresponding piece of it I love, and that makes up, in large part, the core of how I wish to live my life. For instance, I love sewing. I love my sewing machine, a Singer 660 with thirty-three stitch options and a translucent spool. I love mechanically winding the thread, looping it through the thises and thats, snapping the empty bobbin into place, pressing the pedal, and watching the thread swell on the spool—so fast—you can see the accumulation of color, the single strand of blue now a bundle of blue, ready to be clicked into the contraption and threaded through the needle. I love fabric. My favorite brand is Moda, which makes, in addition to unusual designs, vintage children prints, prints at once sentimental and haunting: a girl with curly golden hair offers a boy a frog, and Humpty Dumpty sits on his wall while the letter *w* sprouts wings and flies over the Land of Nod.

But it doesn't end there. I will try to be brief, although it is difficult to cut a passion short. I also love my red enamel colander, my two very domesticated dogs, my pine and Pergo floors, my slotted spoon, my loomed pastel pot holders, and my salad bowl made of lathed and oiled wood. I love my crochet hook, my knitting needles, my Mod Podge glue, and my stencils. I love my steam cleaner and I can get very happy filling it with water, hearing it hiss as it heats up, and then, cloth in hand, firing at the floor, the loud blast of sound always accompanied by a billow of burning mist that dissolves the dirt faster than you can say *Bounty: The quicker picker-upper.*

While I was picking my child up from school recently, Rosemary, one of the other mothers, and I began talking. Many of the mothers who are there for pick-up work in corporate jobs. That day, Rosemary, the CEO of a company, was telling me of her neighbor, an old lady gifted in almost every "domestic art." "We don't do domestic arts in our house," Rosemary said, "so my kids are curious about her."

Domestic arts. That's the term Rosemary used. She didn't say it condescendingly, but it is impossible for a woman to use that phrase in a neutral way while standing in a business suit. "I can't cook," Rosemary said. "I can't even thread a needle," she added, laughing, and I wondered what she would think if I said I could, and often did, in lieu of paying work. The sewing, perhaps I could tell her about the sewing, but the decoupage I knew would remain a deep, deep secret, as would the crocheting, the appliquéing, the stenciling, and the steamer.

What am I hiding, and why? My domestic life is not dumb. It holds within it my writing and rugosa roses, tadpoles as thick as thumbs swimming in the fishbowl on the white windowsill of my daughter's room. Often she and I will go out walking. Now that it is fall, the weather is perfect for this, the sunshine slanting, the air cool. My daughter is six. We pass Colonials, Victorians, vinyl-sided pastiches that tilt and probably leak. I teach her about mansards and hipped roofs and gambrels. This to me is not idle knowledge. If you know what to call a house, from which style it springs, the materials that make up its shape, you know something about how to design and inhabit a life.

And yet too often, late at night, when I find myself involved in a domestic task while my husband reads his chemistry book, I become angry. "Here I am," I think, "pushing the vacuum around and around while he sits with his fat feet up on the table." A thought like this leads me lockstep to a cascade of other thoughts and images—images of men and their dirty underwear on the floor, images of me paying the bills, doing the doctor's appointments, walking the dogs, picking up poop, scooping the coiled mound of excrement into a produce bag. When my husband offers to help in any of these chores (except poop pickup, for which he has never offered help), I say no. Traditional interpretation: I am trying to maintain control, protect my female turf. But, in fact, it's both more and less complex than that. I say no because, even though I feel angry over the fact that I am vacuuming, I also really like my vacuum. It's an Electrolux Harmony with a HEPA filter and an impressively quiet motor. The crevice tool locks into corners and cracks you never even knew existed and sucks out the detritus with a crackling sound as the stuff swirls in the vacuum's lungs, coming to rest at last in the bag bloated with filth. I even like the bag; I like holding in my hands the exact cubic volume of scum and hair packed into one place, one lobe, heavy, somehow significant. "See," I always say to my husband, holding out the bag before I toss it, "see what we live in?" and I have to say, he always looks impressed, and vaguely disturbed.

It is a night in early October. The day shuts down quickly now, shutters banging across the blue, darkness drawn in. The children are asleep, as are the dogs. My Electrolux Harmony purrs from room to room while my husband reads, thoughtfully chewing a pen. And even though I'm having a grand old time, I do what I often do when I look up and see him oblivious to this work. I abruptly switch off the motor and stand staring at him as he sits in the dining room, his fat feet up, my arms akimbo.

"What?" he says.

"Do you realize this is the third time I've vacuumed this week?" I say.

"Um . . . no," he says.

"And today I took Clara to the dentist, plus I got her socks and underwear, plus I made her a new skirt, plus I patched the wallpaper in the bathroom."

He doesn't say anything. He never does. What should he say? What can he say? I know his real thoughts on the subject; he has expressed them to me many times. "So don't vacuum," he'll say. "Did I ask you to vacuum? Do I care whether the wallpaper is patched?" For god's sake, he has told me over and over again, he is a modern man; he asks none of this from me; he would rather me grow hair on my legs and smoke dope all day while writing my own version of "Kubla Khan," better that than, for god's sake, a *wife*. With a *steamer* she holds like a gun.

What do I want from him? Sometimes I want help. More often I want just a certain kind of comprehension, an understanding that, like any other pursuit, the domestic arts are a combination of mindless tasks and mindful executions. Have you ever tried to design a really first-rate quilt? It boggles the brain. It takes a brain. Two years ago I was a Knight Science Journalism fellow at MIT. A part of my research appointment involved going to twice-weekly seminars where I heard researchers speak on topics that ranged from dark matter to the fate of Venice in an era of global warming. Halfway through the year, as the weather got cold, I began to bring my knitting. I knew this would be, at MIT, an act more radical than freeing a pathogen from a locked lab. I did it anyway, with equal parts fear and a desire to get the baby blanket done. On this particular day, Craig Venter was speaking about the genome. The director of the fellowship glared at me as I removed my materials and began to very quietly click away. This was definitely not okay. It was okay for fellows to fool with their wi-fi while listening to a lecture, to IM a colleague across town, to doodle intricate overlapping hexagons on graph paper, but for me to purl in such a situation? Never.

But I digress. Our kitchen table: Twice my daughter fell from the high chair needed to reach its surface. Then, when my son turned one and a half, he discovered the table had wheels, and we came home from work one day to find he had made a sort of sleigh out of it, tying the table to the dogs with ribbon and getting them to pull it like reindeer around our house. This was not a good situation for our dogs, who are old and have hip dysplasia. It presented other dangers as well. I won't get into those here. My husband and I agreed that the table, despite its spectacular storage space and its ability to diminish bills, had to go.

His requirement: that the replacement table be of normal height and have no wheels. My requirement: that the replacement table have built into it both a drawer—the drawer of denial, I call it—and a cabinet in which to store the crock-pot. Such a table, I soon learned, does not exist. Why not, then, build one? I can sew, I can stencil, I can knit. I know flour and grease, stripper and stencils. I know wool, so why not wood? I can use scissors, so why not a saw? In the hardware store I found a circular saw and lifted it up. Its heft was substantial, its teeth bared.

Home Depot is a fine place, especially late at night. The big lights blaze in the warehouse while below thousands of nails twinkle in their assorted bins. I began to go there after I'd put my son to bed. I bought my material: four hefty legs, pre-primed planks of pine wood. It took weeks to assemble everything, and over those weeks, I slowly got to know the immense store. Home Depot has its own code of etiquette. It's okay to stop someone in an aisle and ask whether or not he thinks a shank or a dowel would do a better joinery job. You can discuss for at least half an hour the merits of a brad-point bit versus a blunt-point bit. You can talk about toothless chucks and collets, chamfered dowels and dovetails. It was exhilarating, all these new and mysterious words, as good as pig Latin, a secret society. I bought myself a leather toolbelt and wore it slung low around my hips. Like a secret cross-dresser, I never actually wore it out; I tried it on over and over again behind closed doors, angling myself this way and that in front of the mirror, thinking, "Hmmmm."

I remember one night in particular. It was raining, and the rain made a clattering sound on the tin-topped roof of the store. I thought I might need a table saw in order to make this kitchen table, which was still in the planning stages. And as I stood there with the salesperson discussing the pros and cons of different table-saw brands, an entire group of late-night contractors formed around us, offering their own opinions: "Porter-Cable ten-inch with the rip fence just isn't going to last you" . . . "A Bosch is superior" . . . "Without a dado blade the saw is useless" . . . "What about beveled cuts? Only a Delta can do that." Around and around the men went, discussing the merits of their tools with such genuine feeling I was charmed. They didn't sound dumb or parodically male at all. They sounded thoughtful. The language of their lives rolled off their tongues, as curvaceous as any French. "So which one do you want?" the salesman finally asked me.

I shrugged, scrubbed my eyes with the palms of my hand. "Decisions, decisions," I said.

"You look tired," one of the men said.

"All day with the kids," I said. Somehow, I expected this comment would drive some sort of wedge between me and the men, but it didn't.

"I've got seven myself," the salesman said.

"Your wife work?" I asked.

"Don't have a wife," he said.

"Oh," I said.

He smiled at me. "I think I have the perfect table saw for you out back," he said. "Sit," he said, gesturing towards the orange cart used to haul around lumber. I sat and he hauled me to the back of the store, to the saw he thought I should see. He was my very own workhorse, my coach, my carriage, my prince; I was being treated just like a woman and just like a man at the same time. This, I discovered, was nice.

In woodworking, you have to cut a corner in order to make one. You have to measure out a perfect forty-five degree angle, slice sideways with a hand as steady as a surgeon's, and then mate one mitered corner to another. If you do it wrong, the corner edges will gape and wobble; if you do it right, then you experience something akin to relief, even joy, as the two pieces kiss and click.

I began my work. I moved all the lumber into our dining room and started to figure things out. This, I discovered, was not so easy. Problems I'd never anticipated immediately arose. Wood warps when you clamp it, for one. A straight line is exceedingly hard to create. Most baffling of all, How do you join one board to another? The miter is one way. But as I soon learned, there are also rabbet joints, butt joints, biscuit-joined joints, dowel joints, slot joints, finger joints, and dovetails. This, to me, had philosophical as well as practical implications. Woodworking seemed to be in part an optimistic pursuit, a pursuit that took its cues from E. M. Forster, or perhaps vice versa: connect. Only connect.

What I learned was that woodworking is intensely lyrical, and thus I came to love it. At the same time, it secretes its own power. It's impossible to feel anything but tough when holding a reciprocating saw and wearing a tool belt. The day I bought the reciprocating saw I took my six-year-old out into the backyard with me. The leaves littered the ground like Chanukah gelt, all gold and wet. "What are we going to do?" she asked. "It's a surprise," I said.

I took her over to a tree that had grown so large its branches cast shade over half our yard, turning what was once a perennial garden into a thicket of weeds. "Watch this," I said, and with comic-book flair I held the saw up like a sword, flicked its "on" switch, and brought the roaring machine down to the tree's trunk. It made a jagged quick bite and spun sawdust into the air. The interior of the trunk was pale, and this somehow made me sad. I kept going. As the tree began to tip I told her: "Run!" That was just the beginning. There were other trees to clear. There was other work to do. I bought six-inch screws and sunk them deep into the table's legs. Slowly, like a foal struggling to stand, the table eventually found its footing.

The built-in drawer and cabinet were definite challenges. For these I needed a router, a machine that dervished across a plank of wood, its bit bearing down creating a neat groove into which you can slide shelves. I went early one morning to Rockler, a high-end construction store, where a sales assistant named Woody with an actual wooden leg discussed with me the differences between router bits and bases. "The most important thing," said Woody, "whether you're gang routing, plunging, using jigs, or just doing dadoes, the most important thing is how you use your clamps." I nodded solemnly. "I've been doing this for thirty-five years," said Woody, "and I've always said of all the power tools out there, the human machine's the most dangerous of them all."

My husband began to get seriously impressed when I brought the router home and showed him how to use it. "Why," I asked, "are you so impressed with this but not with my sewing machine?"

My husband likes to theorize about many things, whether he is familiar with them or not. Lately he has theorized about avian flu, Naloxone, and learning disabilities. His theorizing often sets off a fight: How can he know so much about something he has never really researched? "I can have opinions," he says.

But about the router/sewing machine conundrum he had no opinions. He seemed genuinely stumped, as was I. "A sewing machine is just as cool as a router," I said.

"I know, I know," he said.

"But a router has more status, because it's associated with men's work."

"I'm sure that's true," he said. "But it doesn't really have to be men's work anymore. Now that there are all these power tools, you don't need the same kind of upper-body strength to do it."

"Well, then," I said, "why aren't there more women doing it?"

Later on I called Home Depot. The marketing department told me that indeed there are more women getting involved in woodworking. "Ten years ago, our customer base was almost exclusively male. Now it's fifty-fifty," a representative told me. Similarly, a marketing representative at Lowe's, Home Depot's main competition, says their store was designed specifically to attract the female customer. Is this the result of women's changing status, their rise to power, their willingness to enter into and master male-dominated activities? That would be the obvious interpretation. My guess is a little bit different. As my husband, Benjamin, said, power tools have made it so that carpentry does not require the same kind of physical strength it used to. We associate power tools with ultimate machismo, but the reality may be that at a deeper level these ultramasculine tools have feminized and will continue to feminize the craft so that in two decades, three decades' time, a woman with a circular saw will be as common as a woman with a Singer. Even at their most substantial, hand-held power tools do not weigh much more than five pounds, which is less than the satchels stuffed with groceries I must lug up the long stone steps of my house. My son weighed ten pounds when he was born. I carried him around for months, and I didn't even have to use my hands.

From my six-year-old daughter I am newly aware of how the world is divided up between "boy things" and "girl things." Color is the most obvious and perhaps the saddest example of this, because blue is the sky, the sea, the eye, the music. A girl should feel she can claim blue and a boy should know that the raw pink of a wound or the hot pink of hilarity is also his. When it comes to crafts, how, I wonder, did the divisions occur? Why did sewing wind up women's work while wood stayed in the circle of men? Yes, there is the factor of upper-body strength, but that explains only a part of it. After all, wood whittling requires nothing more than a pen knife, and yet I've never seen any women wood whittlers. In images of the eighteenth century the wood whittlers seemed to be all boys, shepherds with time to spare or monks carving frivolous images into prayer stalls as a way of alleviating the stern sobriety of their pious lives.

Perhaps the answer to the wood/fabric conundrum lies in the status accorded to the materials in question. Wood has always been a prized commodity. There was purpleheart, coromandel, sandal-wood, zebrawood, brazilwood, and the rich, dark wood called bois du roi. In the Middle Ages, wood was precious, its production precarious, its artisans granted, therefore, respect. Later woodworkers were seen as artists, employed by kings and the upper crust, their styles shaping their centuries. There were Grinling Gibbons, Duncan Phyfe, Thomas Chippendale, George Hepplewhite, Thomas Sheraton. The last of these, Sheraton was a bitter, boastful man who loved ingenuity above all else. Furniture made by Sheraton was often fitted with secret, spring-action drawers. He designed a bed disguised as a bookcase, a desk with a rolling top.

Theories are one way to give your work, indeed your life, the kind of context it needs to be nuanced and rich, if not in money, then in meaning. In theories, true or not, I can find a way of elevating and explaining my various pursuits, of giving them an intellectual edge no knife or needle can carve. But in the very end, a theory cannot compete with the tactile. Knowing the physics of heat cannot warm you like a blanket or a house.

It has been three months now since I have completed our kitchen table. It is fully functioning, child-friendly, abundant in storage, and white. I painted it with milk-white paint and then stamped its rim with suns the size of quarters. My husband likes to make fun of the table. "It's a great table," he says, "so long as you don't lean on it too hard."

"You're just jealous," I said to him the other night, and, indeed, I believe he is.

But all in all, woodworking has brought us closer together, and in a marriage strained by various competing demands, I am grateful for this. After the table, I built several other, smaller projects, a rocking horse for my son, a blackboard for my daughter. With my husband, I am able to discuss angles, drafting, support studs, the complexity of a curve in a way I have never been able to before. It seems a kind of conversation has opened up. Last night he showed me how to draft a diamond, which is not as easy as it sounds. There we stood, together, in the basement light, he holding the pencil, making the measurements, each side symmetrical, perfect. I took his diamond drawing and traced it onto a plank of pine. Later on today I will take a jigsaw and cut this solid shape, which will be ours.

And what for? For the headboard of the bed I am making us. A new bed, because the old one is busted.

My husband and I speak often about how to best make our bed. The basement is lit by a single low lamp. It is late, late at night. Together we puzzle out the pieces. Canopies, pencil posts, platforms, there are many possibilities. We could discuss it for a long, long time.

And so we do. We stand in the basement in the night with the mice and the cat and the scent of sawdust, and we discuss the rout, the carving. As for myself, I think I have finally found a craft of which I am unashamed, a craft with all the trappings of masculinity and all the intent of domesticity, for what else does the woodworker build if not shelter, if not a place to put your head? As for my husband, I think he has found just the opposite, a way to enter into domesticity without suffering shame, or boredom. As for both of us, we have used these tools to get to a different place, a place neither male nor female—or both. In the end, carpentry is not about power: carpentry is joinery, bringing the beams together, mating the miters. We are learning: dadoes, dovetails, rabbets, blind splines—tongue and groove.

16

Boneyard

Consider this a kind of consumer report. I am not a car gal; I have little interest in vehicles, and the ones that I have owned I've owned until their grisly deaths—burst gas lines, generator poof-outs, whole-engine cardiac arrests requiring that the massive mechanical muscle be lifted from its steel cavity and dropped into a junkyard heap. It's not easy, by the way, to dispose of a dead car. It is easier to dispose of a dead body. Where humans are involved there are also coroners, but when a machine is in question, especially a two-ton one, it is hard to get it off your hands, or out of your yard.

In my case, my little white Hyundai died at seventy-five thousand miles, died beyond repair or resuscitation. I paid a few hundred dollars to get a replacement title and have the car hauled off to the junkyard on a sunny autumn day, the crisp, clear kind when the light is so bright the scrap metal glitters and the gutted tires give off the smell of heated rubber. I watched them finish off my car in that junkyard. The crane took what seemed to be only one small swift bite and it all came crashing down, came down as dust and seat stuffing and shattered glass and rainbow streaks of oil dripping from the pile. I was sad to see the vehicle go. I had bought that car brand new twelve years before for four thousand dollars. That car had carried me through my thirties and into my early forties. With it went a lot of time, a lot of books dreamed up behind its sticky wheel, a lot of babies crying and hauled wood and late-night conversations with my sister, who has since moved to Japan.

I miss my sister. I never envisioned she would spend her midlife years in Osaka, eating seaweed and teaching ESL. When I first bought my car, my sister was in her twenties, with beautiful long, brown hair and a whole career in front of her. Her plan: to get her PhD and teach gender studies in some suave city like Boston, where she could occasionally contribute smart, iconoclastic essays to smart, iconoclastic academic reviews, like *Agni*. She did get her PhD, but she didn't get the college teaching job she'd hoped for. In that she is very much like the rest of us. She has achieved some of what she wanted, and in other ways, she has missed her mark. Her boyfriend's name is Turu. She met him last summer when she was teaching in Osaka. Turu is a businessman. He works for Sony and, as is common in his culture, he foresees a lifelong allegiance to the corporation. That my sister will marry a man so wedded to bureaucracy seems sad to me, almost as sad as the death of my car, which is also from another part of the world and inspired by an Asian spirit.

When my sister first told me of her decision to marry Turu and live in Osaka, she started to cry. This was maybe six months ago, when my car still had some vim, some vigor. She told me of her choice while we were seated in it. The engine was running. It was a soft, new spring night with dew glittering on the ground. "You know what I'm most afraid of?" she said.

"What?" I said.

"I'm most afraid of being buried on another continent. I can't believe the whole family, all you guys, will be buried here, in Boston, and I'll probably be buried in Japan, with Turu and his family."

"Well," I said, "I guess you could have your body shipped back to Boston for burial. That's not out of the question, is it?"

"But then I would be buried in America, and I'd be so far from Turu!" she said, and she started to cry harder. This all seemed a little absurd to me but, at the same time, absolutely apt.

"Well," I said, trying again, "why don't you have Turu agree to be buried in Boston, with you and your family. I mean," I said, "it's the least he could do. You're agreeing to live your life in his fucking country. He could agree to do his death in yours."

"I guess so," she said.

"Let's go," I said.

"Where to?" she said.

We were idling in front of her apartment building. "Blue Shirt," I said, which is a great café near Harvard Square, every wall a different color: mango, melon, grape, avocado. The place pulses. The foods are fresh. With every bite of a Blue Shirt meal, you feel yourself slip into youthfulness.

I have tracked my maturation by my car-repair schedule. Every three thousand miles, when it is time to change the oil, I have also regularly scheduled a teeth cleaning. At thirty thousand miles, when it was time to replace the clutch, I figured I had better go see the eye doctor. When the car hit fifty thousand miles, I hit thirty-five and got my first bone-density test, because my bones have always been thin and brittle. The bone-density test came back with bad news. I needed calcium like a car needed gas: keep it coming. Now that my car is gone, dead, I wonder what is next on my health-maintenance schedule. Lately I have been seeing a lot of TV ads for caskets. Perhaps I should buy one. I am forty-two. My sister now lives in Osaka, a wide, windy continent away, a place as seemingly distant from me as death itself, a place that feels lonely, Osaka. I wish she would come home; I wish I could wake up one night and see her coming home, over the clouds, propelled by my shining white Hyundai, mysteriously resurrected, puff puffing across the enormous blank and black expanse of sky.

I junked my Hyundai two weeks ago. And because I have always calibrated my life to my car's life, I also looked into burial plots for myself. According to my sister, with whom I spoke in Osaka, our family does have its own burial plot somewhere in Brookline, Massachusetts, just outside Boston. I vaguely remember that my grandmother, who lived to the ripe old age of ninety-six, was buried there a few years ago. I drove out there—not in the Hyundai, of course, but in my husband's red Jeep, which is astonishingly, aggressively healthy, what with its four-wheel drive and humongous tires and hemoglobin color. The graveyard was surrounded by a wrought-iron fence and had a wispy, rusted Star of David perched on a pole by the entry gate. I found my grandmother's grave. It was winter then, charcoal coming in by five o'clock, the sun sinking into a flaming slit and gone in four seconds flat, the world yanked back into desolate darkness. And I stood there in the desolate late-day northeast winter darkness, by my grandmother's grave, and sure enough, just as my sister had said, there was a bulging apron of unused land around her headstone, room enough for half a dozen coffins, my mother and father, my two sisters, my brother, me. But what about my husband, my children? There wasn't room for them. And did I really want to be buried next to my mother? We don't get along that well. I decided I would find an alternative.

Still, I lay on the ground in the space I imagined had been reserved for me. This is as morbid as it gets. The ground was hard and freezing. Up above, the moon hung like a yellow earring fastened to the side of the sky. Because it was cold, the air was clear, and the galaxies glimmered, the light millions of years old. I lay not in my grave but on my grave, and I was surprised by how unremarkable it seemed. I had always envisioned death—and the transition into it—as fraught and florescent, the last moments, whether they came in a flaming airplane or in an oncology ward, soap opera-ish in their import, saturated with significance, good-bye. Good-bye. But it occurred to me that when I am lying on my death bed I might find the process banal, as much a part of ordinary life as leaving for overnight camp, a trip taken, ultimately manageable, far

more dreaded than dreadful. Someday I will die, just like my car. Maybe I will go to heaven and be reunited with my car. I doubt it. I don't doubt I will die, but it just might be that the passage is unremarkable, a train taken, a candle blown, my very last nanosecond spent thinking, "This isn't nearly as scary as I thought. I wish I'd worried less."

Yes.

Rest your head.

Of course I have no way of knowing, and when the time comes, during which I will be availed of that information, I will have no way of reporting back to you, I'm sorry to say. I would like most of all to write an essay about how it is to die. This would surely win me the Pulitzer for, among other things, reporting. But my skills extend only so far. How far? I will never win the Pulitzer. I will never crawl my way into the canon, where Virginia Woolf lives. Midlife has its revelations, and this is one of them—not what you will do but what you won't do; not how far you will go but how far you can go, and no further. Once I hoped to be brilliant. I hoped to be a female Faulkner. Once, the fact that I was not a female Faulkner was agonizing to me. Now, in middle age, I accept this; I take what I can get. I cherish my oil changes; I am grateful for brakes that work, a brain that works; I respect that I may not be a brilliant novelist but that I have become, after a lot of hard work, a writer, capable of chugging along, capable of crafting a story with a well-made engine, I write Ford or Pontiac paragraphs; they are decent, smart enough, but they are not Mercedes-Benz, Rolls Royce, Cadillac kinds of paragraphs, not top of the line. Not even close.

The death of my car prompted me to find my burial site and then reject it. It also prompted me to some philosophical musings about the passage of time and so on. At its most mundane level, it prompted me to buy a new car because I was still alive, still here, still transportable across the time/space continuum. Now, to me, buying a new car holds about as much interest as buying a new boiler. I began

to desultorily search through the classifieds. New? Used? Newly used? Gently used? Used up? To get a really good car I saw, immediately, would cost me half a year's salary—or more! I could get a Hummer for forty thousand dollars. I briefly, oh so briefly considered it. Imagine living my life with a Hummer at my side. Imagine the shining purple armor of its exterior, its gargantuan wheels crushing weather and stone; its windows, whisper-sliding up and down in their oiled slits, so clear, that glass so tough it wouldn't shatter. Imagine being so safe. So high off the ground. I briefly wondered: Was I a Hummer gal? Could I become one? How would I have to change my wardrobe to fit a Hummer image? Was a Hummer gal sleek, with frothy expensive scarves wound around her neck? Or did she wear Frye boots? This is not important, the specifics. What is important is that I briefly considered it. Options unfolded like rooms in a dream. I could go Hummer. I could go Porsche. I could go Cadillac or junk or Prius. I could operate on hydrogen, electricity, diesel, or gas. There are many ways to power a motor. There are all sorts of lifelines.

I went to a car agency. I had a cold, the kind that makes your throat feel raw and your sinuses inflamed and illuminated on your face, like the person in the Dristan commercial. With such a cold it seems the skin has thinned and your interior is exterior, with all its flaws and germs. Honking into wadded tissue, I told the salesman what I needed. I said, "I need a new car." This is apparently as ridiculous as saying to a doctor that you need a new body. The car salesman, who was sitting in a faux-paneled office, looked up at me, chewing on the pink teat of a pencil eraser. "New car?" he said. He had a wicked, slow smile. "V8 or V6, cloth or leather, all power, standard, antilock, tilt seats, cruise control, color . . ." He ticked off the options, very few of which I understood. Suddenly I felt mad. My nose was burning. "Car," I said. "Tires, steering wheel, seat."

The car salesman had a bowl on his desk and inside there was a bright fish swimming about. The bottom of the bowl was covered in heartbreakingly blue pebbles, a kind of pure blue, as though its color had been sucked straight from the sky. Also in there was a plastic castle and some plastic fronds, which the dumb fish kept trying to nibble. My heart went out to that animal. It had slits in its side, slits that pulsated, showing dark shadows beneath the golden skin. I did something strange then. I reached over, grabbed the jar of fish food, and sprinkled some in. The car salesman looked at me, an eyebrow raised. "I feel bad for your fish," I said. "Your fish is living a miserable life."

"How do you know?" the car salesman said.

Now, this was not the sort of response I expected from a car salesman. It seemed a simple question, but anyone could hear how it reverberated with concerns about consciousness, the possibility of interspecies empathy, whether one can ever acquire experience beyond the circle of self. "I guess, I don't know for sure," I said. "But the question is, really, does the fish know?"

The salesman looked in at the fish. He tapped his pink eraser on the bowl. The fish, who was hoovering up the flakes floating on the water, suddenly darted away, then hunched at the bottom of the bowl.

"The fish knows," I said.

The car salesman sensed he had a loony tune on his hands, or, better yet, a loony tune who had not done her homework. He suggested to me a car with a strange-sounding Arabic name, a Yemeni or something like that, massive, four-door, with a dashboard it would have taken a tech school education to interpret. I knew as soon as I saw the Yemeni that it was not my car, not my life, but I agreed to test it anyway. I hurt my back trying to get in. When you are in your forties, your back becomes your front; you feel it all the time, it snaps and whistles as though it is possessed of intestines. In my case, I have occasional sciatica.

I turned the key in the ignition and the car did not so much roar as whoosh into life. It was a sunny day, our own sun, a star in midlife, burning in the blue. The car salesman had fastened a license plate to my prosthetic butt and I sped down the road, all new and huge, my name not Lauren but Jeb11. As Jeb11 I felt groundless. I felt like a fish in a broken bowl. The glass cracks and suddenly all the world is yours, if you can breathe it in. As Jeb11, in Jeb11, I saw the streets spiraled out across the world and I could, if I wanted to, drive and drive. I could steal this car in a snap. I could go to Vermont, or Oregon. I could feed any fish I wanted. I could stop writing and become a painter. I could sell houses in Silicon Valley. I could swim with the dolphins and feel their suede-gray skin set everything in its place, right the tilt to the world. As Jeb11 I saw the truth as it exists for women like me in today's day and age. I may be dying, but I am also just coming alive. In 2005, my chances of living another forty-two years were pretty good. Now I'm sure I've jinxed myself and that I'll be dead tomorrow, knock wood. But I no longer need be superstitious now that I'm forty-two. I can take testosterone and grow zits and muscles; I can take estrogen and brightly bleed. I can join a gym. I can play the piccolo. I am in my midlife, and this has many possible meanings, one of which is that the glass is half full.

In any case, I did not buy the Yemeni because, in both the long and short run, I am not Jeb11. I decided on a used car, one that would allow my kids a college education. Besides, there was no need to rush what was fast becoming an enlightening experience of self-redefinition. Why should I buy a new car when I am used? Shouldn't a used person get a used car? Should not a car reflect who you are, not who you wish to become? Yes, yes. Of course.

Not far from where I live is a used-car lot with a shack slumped at the side, and on the shack a sign saying "Charlie's." I'd seen this place for years but never had I considered that someday I might go there. I went there. The cars were crammed into the lot, so you had to pick out the aisles between them and squeeze through. Every sales tag pasted on every windshield had an exclamation point after its price. Every car sported a sporty flag, red or green, snapping in the wind, lending the vehicles a feeling of animus, as though they might begin to tap-dance on their tires. Charlie was a pudgy, mustached man who spoke mostly Portuguese, which seemed for some strange reason to enhance our communication rather than limit it, despite the fact that I speak no Portuguese. I speak only English. In high school I took German, French, and Latin, and in elementary school I knew Hebrew, but those languages have vanished from my life, leaving barely a trace of their shapes, a ghostly half-fogged alphabet. I know this because recently I have tried to reclaim my languages. I tried reading a child's book in German, a book that once would have been well below my Brecht reading level, and practically the only words I recognized were *Welt* and *Kindergarten.* I tried reading Camus in French, something that was once a breeze for me, and the little black words squirmed all over the page like parasites. People say that once you learn a language you retain its traces in your gray matter, a kind of print in perpetuity, a cortical calligraphy. This is not true for me. If my brain ever had a forever archive, a little locked trunk where feathers and fantasies and memories and words were stored in an air-tight space, that trunk itself is gone now. Things disappear. Whole languages go back into the black hole that is your head. If you look at a picture of brain cells, you can see there are spaces between the synapses, little slits like trash chutes in apartment buildings.

Charlie was speaking to me in Portuguese and pointing to a teal-green Subaru, a car that appeared very relaxed, like a green lizard snoozing in the sunshine on the lot. The sign in the windshield said seventy thousand miles, three thousand dollars. At one point, when I was thirty-three, seventy thousand miles would have been too much for me. Who would buy a car on its last legs? But that was when I was thirty-three, almost a decade ago, and time has a way of altering its values. When I was six, twenty-six was impossibly old. Now that I'm forty-two, seventy is spry! I try to convince myself of this. If there was ever a need to learn physics, it occurs at midlife. All those questions about traveling in a rocket ship at the speed of light, gone for what seemed like two seconds, only to return to earth and find that thousands of years have passed, and you are alone—this is a midlife metaphor. How can time move so fast and so slow? Why do a feather and a stone fall at exactly the same rate? Am I feather or a stone, and does it matter if the plummet is singularly so swift? What is a light year? What is light? What is a quark? I have begun to sense the utter oddity of the natural world. Nothing is what it seems. Stare for a long time at your yellow wall.

It dissolves into thousands of pieces of particles, and the yellow itself breaks down, releasing its compressed components of bright white and lime green and purple. The world comes apart, and it is lovely.

This time, I did some research. My friend Elizabeth had a Subaru, and she said it was a great car, even though she gave it up for a mini-van. *Consumer Reports* gave the Subaru five stars, except for the 1988 Brighten, which had some mysterious steering-wheel malfunction. I test-drove the car. It had a strange murmur in its engine, but Charlie communicated to me that a car murmur is not much different than a heart murmur—no beeg deel. He would have it fixed.

"I want you to change the brake pads, change the oil, get it inspected, check the tires, change all the fluids, and if it pans out, I'll take it." Charlie agreed. I left the lot after that last exchange feeling high and mighty, feeling suave and smart. I drove a hard bargain. I was not to be fooled.

That night, my daughter's hamster, Fid, escaped from his cage, and I rescued him by carving through the heating ducts with a steak knife and yanking him triumphantly from the jagged rip. Before bed, I took out my pastels and used their blunt tips to draw rich blue lines and ochre spirals across the white paper. I went to bed happy. I woke up happy. I thought I could draw the sun; I thought I could see its blackness and its brightness all in one. I went to the bank and got a bank check for three thousand and some odd dollars, and then I brought the check to Charlie, and then I bought the car. A new car! Congratulations!

For three months, I drove it happily. Spring turned to summer turned to fall. In October, the highway shone before me like a swath of hammered silver. The trees on the sides of the road were a deep midnight green; the birds, bright flecks in the branches. The hill before me, suddenly before me, ascended sharply, at its rounded top a soft smudge of clouds. I climbed and climbed. After three good months, I had confidence in that car. I had confidence until the moment I saw smoke tendrilling out from beneath its clamped hood.

"Smoke," I thought. Sometimes you see things and they don't register as they should. I saw the smoke, but I did not react. I marveled at its purple tinges, its wooly texture. Then, in a snap, that smoke turned black, and faster than abracadabra the car caught fire in a sort of vehicular temper tantrum, coming out of nowhere, spewing in public. I didn't have time to be scared. I must have pulled over to the side of the road, although I don't remember doing this. I do remember yanking the hood release, and I do remember that the hood release broke off in my hand.

I stood on the side of the road, then, and watched my new used car burn, holding the hood release, feeling as humiliated as I was frightened. Someone in a passing car must have called the fire department, because I don't have a cell phone. With their tough rubber hoses the firemen smashed the flames flat until all that was left of my purchase was a charred hull. I got it towed. The firemen gave me a ride home. I had never ridden in a fire truck before. I did not feel good about it. The firemen seemed to think the broken hood release was especially funny. One used it as a back scratcher. "Time to get a new car," they said to me. I picked at the canvas skin of a hose coiled next to me. "That *was* my new car," I said. When the fire truck pulled up in front of my house, all my neighbors came onto their porches to see. They did not expect to see me, climbing down the chrome steps, helped by a man in a trench coat and hip-high rubber boots. "Thanks," I said. I waved good-bye using the useless hood release, holding it high.

I wandered around my house for a while after that, dazed, and then I called Charlie. "Too bad," he said to me in what seemed to be remarkably good English, "too bad, but your ninety-day warranty has expired."

Expired. Ninety days. I have been had. I am sucked on, sucked down, sucking, and I cannot stop. If you were to look at the planet Earth from far enough away, you would see the grids of gray land and the haze of creamy clouds, and also you would see what seemed to be snow, an always storm, falling not down but up, and you would wonder why a snowstorm was falling up, a snowstorm that defied gravity, until you realized that was not snow but souls, billions of them every second dying and rising and swiftly being sucked into the atmosphere. And I am mad. I, like my car, have a temper. My husband frequently says he refuses to buy life insurance due to my temper. He is a little afraid I might get mad and shoot him for the money. "But honey," I have tried to explain to him, "that's so premeditated. I'm not the type to kill in a premeditated way. I'm more the type to do it on impulse. So I think you should buy the life insurance."

Charlie, beware. I was mad. I am woman, hear me roar. But the roar was not about gender or rights. It was a roar into the darkness, the cheapness, and the fire. I went to my closet and got all dressed up in my very best suit. I had a plan that I had not really planned. It had just come to me, roaring, an insane inspiration. I would dress up like a lawyer and go down to Charlie's slumped shack, disguised, and do something threatening. But what? I buttoned my whalebone jacket. I zipped up the silk-lined skirt. My heels were high and sharp and sounded like scalpels on the glossy wood floor of my kitchen. This was noontime, the husband at work, the kids in school, no one to witness this insanity. It was insanity, because no matter how much makeup I put on my face, I still looked like Lauren, not a lawyer. There is a great gulf between Lauren and a lawyer, I realized, frantically dabbing foundation on my face, that even Clinique could not bridge.

Eventually I stopped this madness. But I was not calm. My fingers still smelled like soot from the burnt car. A few hours later, towards the end of the day, still dressed as a lawyer but only halfway hidden, I went to the phone and called Charlie.

"Hello," he said.

"This is attorney Frances Bacon from the law firm Cabot, Cabot, and Lowell calling on behalf of my client Lauren Slater."

"Who?" he asked.

"Lauren Slater," I said, and saying it made me real. "Her name is Lauren Slater and she bought a used car from you that caught fire and thus violates statute 345 and 822bca regarding the condition and safety of used vehicles in the state of Massachusetts."

Charlie didn't say anything. I had him, hooked. My hook.

"My client is here with me now and planning to sue for damages on several counts," I said.

"I told her," Charlie said, "I told her, I told her I would take back the car, give her a new one."

"My client reports a very different story," I said.

"I have a nice red station wagon," he said.

"My client demands her money back and five thousand dollars restitution or she will proceed with a lawsuit," I said. I sounded so unlike myself. I sounded so official, so lawyerly, so multivoiced and tonally complex. It was like learning a new way of speaking, new kinds of consonants, knowing all the while the knowledge was friable. I became a lawyer and the lawyer brought me Lauren, with her laws and limits and humor.

The next day, I took my two children, Clara and Lucas, with me to Charlie's to collect my refund plus "bonus." I wanted Charlie to see that he could have killed my kids. Looking back on it now, I see the gesture as melodramatic and insulting, not to any one person so much as to motherhood itself. My kids are beautiful, and they are not symbols but skin. Motherhood, like life itself, is never clearly drawn, while melodrama always is. I had suffered, but so had Charlie, of course. I was a good mother, but I also was not, of course. My kids, in any case, did not cooperate with this ploy. They were obnoxious in the slumped shack. Lucas, my two-year-old, kept trying to honk all the horns. Clara, my six-year-old, kept saying, "Let's get a four-wheel drive!" Lucas found the water dispenser and, unbeknownst to us, turned on the tap and caused a small flood. I left, check in hand, apologizing for my mess. This is as it should be. Strong and sorry both.

I have not yet bought a new car. I am now, thanks to Charlie, five thousand dollars richer than I was. And I don't think I'm going to get a new car after all. I think I'll save my profit and instead use it to get a gown or a motorbike, or take a trip to Osaka, where my sister is living, and dying, eating seaweed, learning a new language that for a short time anyway will not replace the old one; she will have two languages. Two ways of talking. Two different words for grief and gladness, old and young, beginnings and endings. Hello and good-bye.

17

Dolled Up

I have an idea. It's not a new idea, as people from time immemorial have been suggesting that your inner state—happiness, serenity, and so on—depends at least in part on how you look. But I've always disregarded any advice that has to do with sprucing up, preferring to rely, instead, on chemical concoctions to tamp down or even transform my depression, which has been with me for so long now I know it like a friend. My depression, for instance, inhabits my heart and takes the shape of a small speckled stone worn smooth by my body's currents, its contours changing over time while its weight remains precisely the same. My depression does magic. Poof! It always, reliably, disappears around four or four thirty in the afternoon and then slam! Bam! It returns each day at dawn, settling in all morning and for much of the afternoon, sapping my energy, stealing colors from trees and leaves and socks and spoons, so even my miniature teacup, a relic from centuries past and painted the most delicate resonant yellow, even that falls flat while I watch my world drain down and out until, in the end, everything looks like a carbon copy of what it once was, still and silent, as if under some spell.

I'm not complaining, or if I am I don't mean to be. Thanks to antidepressants I now have seven hours more or less of good, clear time, and I try to use it well, ticking off items on my to-do list, trying to tie up my business, so when disability comes at least my things will be in order. Still, seven waking hours is not a lot, a mere fraction of the fifteen or so most "normal" people have in a day. Last year I spent eighty dollars on a huge silver-rimmed clock from Pottery Barn, the kind of clock they once had in old-fashioned train stations, with big black hands and ticks so loud it's as if each one comes with its very own exclamation point. My family complains about my clock, which I have hung in the hub of our house, the library, the place for play and reading, but I need it there, right where I can hear it best, a constant reminder of my dilemma and its demands.

Given my very tight timeline, it should come as no surprise that many things in my life fall to the wayside. My taxes, for instance, are always, always late. I cannot indulge in frippery and frills, in long soaks in a tub full of beads or bubbles, or spritzes of perfume pumped from a crystal bottle, the mist landing lightly on the pulse in the nook of the neck. I do not adorn myself, no necklaces or bracelets, no earrings, despite the fact that each lobe is perfectly pierced. I shop for my children's clothes, flying through Target as fast as I can, ripping from the racks the pants and shirts and skirts that society demands they wear. As for myself and what I wear? I'm embarrassed to say. Right now I'm dressed in a pair of pajama-like pants, the hems frayed, the elastic gone loose at the waist so the pants slump down and sit on my very abundant hips. On top I'm wearing a floppy gray shirt stained here and there with various seepages and spills. My hair is two-toned; the bottom, an anemic yellow—think faded paper, think sepia. The "roots" are now halfway down my head, wiry grays, the occasional silky dogwood-white. On the windowsill in the bathroom sits an unopened box of colorant, "pure brown" the box reads, while pictured above the words is a woman with hair seal-smooth and swinging. I keep meaning to dye my strands, but I never have the time unless, of course, I could somehow make use of those stone-still hours of grief that daily descend on me, sending me straight to my bed, a quilt over my head.

The truth of the matter is I'm a schlump, a frump, my clothes second-hand and utterly without style, dirt in my otherwise nacreous nails, like a line of toner at the base of the beds, the nails themselves without shape, their excess hacked off every few months, making my already stubby fingers look still more so. Once, what seems like many moons ago, a publicist insisted I purchase an Ann Taylor suit for a CNN interview about a book I'd recently written. I remember the mall, empty that Sunday morning, and in the store how the tiny suit fit my then-tiny form just so, making me look more like a lawyer than the frumpy writer I was. For a while I loved that suit and even wore it around the house, but, like most transformations, it all went up in dust after the novelty wore off, and the suit was retired to the back of my paint-peeled closet, where it hangs today covered in a plastic pouch.

When I look at the suit now, I can't quite believe I once loved it, so distant does it seem from the reality of my life, my body, my shape, radically altered by meds that have packed on fat, the fat abetting me in my utter disregard for personal appearance; why even try? It seems so hopeless. This is why I have never had a pedicure and can't see why I ever would, what with only seven productive hours to my day. My shoes, clogs of some sort that I bought in the bargain bin at CVS, are made of rubber, the insides padded with fake fur grown dirty over time. My heels are exposed, the skin there deeply creased and dead to boot, so that even in the cold of winter I can wear my bargain-bin clogs because my heels are numb to the wind. I once bought a device called "The Egg," shaped like a dome with a raspy underside, its purpose to sand down the hardened parts of a woman's body, the corned feet, the whitened, wizened elbows. I did not buy The Egg out of some desire to preen—not me, no never—but rather because I was curious as to how much dead skin I actually had on my heels, the looks of which I could no longer recall, completely covered with callous. I sat on the edge of my bed, tore The Egg from its packaging, and began to sand myself, watching with amazement as my skin snowed and snowed, and when I pressed down harder on my heel, whole whitened rinds of dead flesh came curling off—utterly painless, and curious too. That skin was so old it could have been from a prior decade, time encased, preserved, the body literally retaining its past. I kept sanding my heels, determined to find the pink part, the snow heaping up at the edge of the bed, and yet no matter how long, how hard I worked, I couldn't get down to fresh flesh. I put The Egg in my bedside drawer. I got a broom and dustpan and swept myself up and into the waste bin.

This is a confession, a way of cleansing myself symbolically, to make up for the fact, perhaps, that in real life I rarely shower. I sometimes smell, and then I shower. I wash my hair with whatever's in the shower stall, most often some fruity concoction for kids. A few months ago I developed an abscess at the base of my spine. At first I thought I'd bruised the coccyx, but weeks went by, the pain only increased, and when I reached my hand around I felt a hot, hard lump weeping fluid clear and odorless. My primary-care physician told me I had what is called a pilonidal cyst, an infection of sorts and a bad one to boot. The next day, lying on my belly on the surgeon's steel table, I had the cyst emptied, a procedure so painful it lies beyond language, the surgeon, with no Novocain, no anesthetic at all ("We just don't use anesthetics for pilonidal cysts"), slicing into the boil and then squeezing its contents so hard I heard the spurt and saw, smeared on a large white cloth, blood and pus and a lot of green goo, the smell fetid and wrong. The surgeon stuffed gauze and a wick into the wound and told me to shower every day, to keep myself as clean as I could, and to come back in two weeks to have the wick removed. On the way out he handed me a prescription for Oxycontin, which I immediately filled and took four of, though the label limited the dosage to two. I lay back on my bed and watched the air swirl and eddy by my head.

I realized, even in my stoned state, that my self-neglect had gone past the point of acceptable. I was now literally getting infected. The surgeon had explained to me that the cyst is caused when a stray piece of dirt works its way under the skin, inflaming it. I realized that, depression or no, I needed to change my ways. I realized I'd have to start devoting some time to grooming, as they say, like a normal person, stepping into the shower in the mornings and coming out with dripping hair and wrapping myself in a soft, floppy towel, depression or no; it didn't matter. I thought of a study I'd read a long, long time ago, so long ago I could no longer recall the paper or book from which this study derived, but the gist of it had stayed with me. This study found that mood is influenced by one's outward appearance, which had seemed odd to me and still seemed odd to me. Mood, so deep and internal, so unrelenting and unyielding: how could a skirt or some flowing fabric possibly shift

that behemoth? And yet the study found that when "ADL skills"—
activities of daily living, such as showering, combing your hair, at-
tending to your skirt and shirt—improved, so too did the symptoms
of depression in the subjects under scrutiny. Of course, it could have
very well been the other way around, that when symptoms of depression improved, the subjects in the study were more motivated
to care for their appearance. I thought of a lake I'd seen last winter,
its surface completely capped with ice through which a lone fisher-
man had drilled a single hole and was hauling up huge trout that
flapped and flopped on the frozen surface. The blood, the slick fish,
the skidding sunlight—it made an impression on me because it suggested that surface and the interior that surface covered were intimately linked, and that one could not exist without the other.

A psychologist by training and degree, I decided, in my stoned
state, my cyst draining into the packed gauze, that I'd construct my
own experiment on the relationship between surface—how you
look, how you appear—and mood, which the surface either en-
hances or hides. I was a schlump, a frump, due to the remnants of
depression that both robbed me of the time to spruce up and the
motivation to do so. Was it possible, though, that, once spruced, my
mood would follow suit? What would happen if during my "down
time" I put on makeup, a swoosh of rouge or thick and black mascara that separated and extended each individual lash, lending my
eyes a depth they didn't really have? What would happen if I got
some sass, some style? Beauty, after all, is not some trifle; rather, it's
a sought-after state in every culture we know of, this in itself proof
of its power. I've seen photos of African women who adorned their
necks with heavy metal rings that, over time, push down their collar bones and compress their ribs, all this for a lengthened neck.
And despite the fact that the practice was banned in 1912, some,
maybe just a few, wealthy Chinese families still bind their daughters' tender feet. The Maori of New Zealand believe beauty is ob-
tained by the intricate scrolls and swirls of tattoos that they pierce
into their skin, while in Mexico and other dark-skinned nations,
skin-whitening products are all the rage, whereas, in our predomi-
nately light-skinned nation, tanning products line the shelves and
tanning salons are everywhere, all this zig and zag proving that

there's nowhere in the world where the concept of beauty does not exist, nowhere that people fail to pay homage to its power.

Being your typical white, middle-class American, I know what beauty means to me, and so I set off to pursue it, but not before constructing for myself some sort of experimental design. The specifics: I'd spruce myself up every day for three weeks and observe whether or not I could alter my inward mood by changing my outward appearance. My resolve to follow this path increased when, that night, I read in our town paper an interesting, relevant ad: a woman named Sally, who called herself a "beauty consultant," offered, for a small fee, to come to your house and teach you how to put your best foot forward, covering everything from makeup to clothes to shoes to hair and its endless shades of color. The ad seemed so tailor-made for me and my situation that I couldn't help but think that providence had placed it in my way. So I called Sally, a peppy-sounding woman who, three days later, pulled into my driveway, her car small and sleek, the trunk popping open just as she stepped out. Walking around to the rear of her car, she pulled out two bulky black cases. I was watching from my kitchen window, but even from this distance I could see that my beauty consultant was impeccably done up, with a black furze of curls and reddened lips, her rayon slacks rustling in the wind, her floral tunic scoop-necked with a big bow in the back. I watched her come up my walkway, those cases swinging in her hands, and that's when I thought, *Oh no.* What was in those cases? Was she some kind of Avon lady carrying a brand of makeup that no one had ever heard of, a "consultant" who would cream up my face with various "products" she'd then try to sell me for a fat fee? The doorbell rang and I opened it with falling faith and stepped back as Sally stepped into my kitchen. Suddenly wary and in no mood to be polite, I immediately said, "What's in the black bags?" and Sally said, extending her hand, "Hi, I'm Sally." Chagrined, just a little, I shook her slender paw, noting her nails, sculpted and painted a pearly pink. She set the cases onto the floor and said, "These? These are my before-and-after photos from various clients I've worked with." I sat with her in the living room, me with my weeping, aching back boil and my dumpy, smelly clothes, and she in a cloud of lilac scent, and we flipped through the photos and designed my own personal program plan. Then Sally stood up, stepping back and scanning me from top to toe, and announced after just a moment's consideration this one word: *Hair.*

Instinctively I put my hand to my hair, felt its brittle, sun-scorched surface, and I nodded in agreement. *Hair.* We started there. Sally made the appointment, some fancy salon, the type I'd never of my own volition set foot inside of, especially because the appointment slot was set for ten o'clock, smack-dab in the middle of my daily despair. So when the day and time for the appointment rolled around, I could barely drag my carcass from my sleep-warmed sheet, where every inch of me longed to stay. I heard my doorbell ring and then, "Yoo-hoo? Yoo-hoooo?" accompanied by the clickety-clack of Sally's stiletto shoes coming to haul my sorry ass out of bed and into the stylist's seat. "I'm not up for this," I said, still prone on my pillow, and she said, "Now you are," finding my arm beneath the blankets and literally pulling me up and marching me towards her car, me, still in my sleepwear, which didn't much differ from my daywear. Once I was in her Honda, Sally shoved my feet into the bargain-bin clogs she'd grabbed on our way out of the house and then said, "Stinko. Shoes are next."

The salon was far away. We drove down highways, over underpasses, and under overpasses, the roads circling and serpentining, the sky above the hard blue of a gem, the salon's parking lot oddly empty, the salon itself in a circular building, all spiral staircases and dizzying display racks of dozens of different shampoos, conditioners, curl creams, mousses, gels, sprays, the air inside scented, water falling from a bank of rocks into a reflecting pool lined with luminous stones so smooth and pearly I wanted only to touch one, to hold it against my heart, as if it might bring comfort, as if I could somehow palm my own pain, and in doing so shape it, or erase it.

Sally knew everyone in the salon, or at least it seemed that way. I was ushered to a changing room, told to take off my top and replace it with a crinkling black gown that snapped shut and then, for extra measure, tied at the waist. The gowns, clearly, were made for slender women, my bulk straining the snaps, so the fabric pulled at my chest and left visible gaps that I wanted to hide with my hands but could not. "Yoo-hoo," Sally called, tapping on the door of the changing room. So out I stepped, into the misty, sweet-smelling humid air, led, then, to a circle of chairs, each one holding a woman dressed in an identical black gown, the women's heads all tipped back into deep basins while slender men worked their scalps into luscious lathers. "This is Albert," Sally said to me, directing my gaze towards the man who would first handle my hair, and I gave him a wary, embarrassed smile. Sally, peppy as ever, patted the seat while Albert held my elbow as I sank into the leather chair and then felt myself tipped backwards into the basin's black bowl, Albert adjusting the water's temperature, suds exploding on my head, and then his fingers, ropy and strong, working the soap through my strands, front to back, tipping me ever so slightly forward to get the fuzz at the nape of my neck, a feeling so fine, this was, my whole scalp kneaded as if it were dough and might rise with just the right type of touch, and so I was soothed. The stone in my heart softened and rocked in a tiny interior tide pool. Behind my closed eyes, fish flickered and fronds bent and went with the waves of light, making swirls and shadows on the insides of my lids. *Comfort.* I hadn't expected to find it here, but here it was, in the soap, the streams, the strength of the fingers moving the skin of my scalp so all the blood pooled at my feet, cold and coagulated, all of it warmed up and came coursing through me, and then he was done and turbaned me with a towel, and I opened my eyes, a single bead of water sliding down the side of my nose, which Albert patted dry so softly with the edge of a terrycloth towel.

Now to the stylist's seat. Andrew, the stylist, looked about sixty years old. "He's the best here," Sally whispered to me, and I nodded but found that fact odd, because Andrew had a whisker-grizzled chin and a head of wild unkempt hair, his shirt untucked and earrings lining the ledge of both ears, tiny stones of red and turquoise, purple and blue. Andrew stood behind my seat and looked at me in the mirror. He then walked around to the front of the seat, knelt, and almost reverentially cupped my face between his two raspy hands, moving my head left, now right, studying something about me but what it was I didn't know. I suddenly felt embarrassed, felt as if he could see past my skin to the dull nothing that made me *me* for so many hours of the day. And as if to confirm that this in fact was true, Andrew suddenly nodded crisply, sprang to his feet, and, without asking me what kind of cut I wanted, picked up scissors that looked preternaturally huge to me, like something out of a storybook, clack-clacking as he aimed them at my locks, which I'd much cared for but now, faced with their demise, suddenly did. "Wait a minute," I said. "Wait, wait." So Andrew stopped in mid-motion, the huge silver scissors frozen and glittering, and I said, "Aren't you going to ask me what I want?"

"You don't know what you want," Andrew said, his eyes piercing and fiercely intelligent. He was correct. I had no idea what sort of style would suit me nor had I had any idea, until now, that I harbored, in some subconscious place, feelings of affection for my hair. "Let me take care of this," Andrew said. "I've been cutting hair for thirty years."

And then he went to work. He dove into me, lifting me up in layers, splicing me sideways, and cutting with complete confidence, long, wet locks falling onto the floor. I eyed them with a rising tide of fear: Would he leave anything at the end? Was his idea to stubble my scalp, so my inside mirrored my outside, a wrecked ruin, not a single softening streak? *Snap snap*, said the scissors, again and again, dark and dripping hanks falling to the floor as Andrew muttered, *Thick*, a remark about my head or my hair, I wasn't sure which. Andrew circled and serpentined, spun me around in my seat, pumped me up, then down, then swung me once more around and then, suddenly, with no slowing, no sense of a conclusion coming, just all of a sudden he stopped. The scissors stopped. My hair, which had before fallen past my shoulders, now came in close to my neck, stopping at the nape, which, for the first time in years was bare and touched by the breezes of many people moving past, the mist in the air landing lightly on me, the air so dewy even my arms were moist.

Andrew circled my seat slowly, slowly, with great ceremony, moving me around until at last I fully faced the mirror and could see what he had done to me, my hair, still damp but drying now, released from the weight of its long length, all cowlicks and curves, my bangs gone, my face in a frame of waves. "You like?" he asked and, then, without waiting for a reply, he took the towel he'd draped around my neck and used it to tousle my locks, saying, as he did, "You won't ever need to blow this style dry." He set the towel down. "Lauren," he said, standing behind me now, leaning in and down so our faces were side by side in the mirror. "Listen to me, Lauren," he said.

"I'm listening," I said, and indeed I was.

He was so close I could smell his cologne. His voice had a commandeering quality. "Lauren," he said again, "you have heavy hair."

I nodded. Sally, standing a little ways off, nodded too.

"All that weight," Andrew said.

I suddenly wanted to weep. It was as if he knew about the stone inside me, as if he were speaking not about my head but my heart.

"I've released you," he said, "from all that weight, and now," Andrew said, suddenly springing up like a jack-in-the-box, "and now, look what we have here." He cupped the back of my head while tweaking a curl, pulling it past its kink, and then letting it loose so it fell back into perfect position. "I'll bet you never knew how stunning you were, under all that weight," Andrew said.

"She is stunning, isn't she," said Sally, smiling, her arms folded across her chest.

"Stunning?" I said. That seemed a bit of an overstatement. I'm forty-nine and lined in all the wrong ways. I'm a good eighty pounds overweight. Stunning, impossible, but improved, that could certainly be. *Weight weight weight*, that word *weight* kept going through my head. And then, suddenly, it was as if everyone had disappeared. I lost the sounds of the salon, the sounds of the waterfall and the cash register, the sounds of hot hair dryers and women whispering. Suddenly there was just me and my mirror, which I now leaned into, my reflection looming up, zooming up, the curls so curly, my hair dark brown veined with a glossy sweet silver, the look light and alive, my face indeed framed, the pink seam of a new side part making my nose and my mouth and my eyes seem somehow softer, with sparkle. I blinked. Still there. I reached up cautiously to touch my hair. Then I put my hand on my still damp head and pressed down, hard, seeing if I could squelch the sudden spirals; they bounced back. They would not be banished. I gave Andrew a twenty-dollar tip.

At home, alone at last, I faced my unmade bed, the sun gushing in through the bank of windows, tree shadows swaying on the floor. I had been lightened of a load, my head, and by extension maybe my mind, as well, restyled. And yet I still felt my stone, only was it, could it be, that it was somehow smaller? I picked up a hand mirror, a flea-market find, silver-backed, pearl-handled, the glass flecked here and there with spots. I brought it to me and, before I could study my brand-new face, I set it down and headed for the bathroom, where I turned on the shower and stood under its spray, the jets of water running down my bare back and clearing it of prickly hairs. Instead of stepping out, I then turned on the tub, shut off the spray, and before long was standing ankle-deep in wet warmth. Slowly, so slowly, I lowered my heft down into the filling cavern, the water roaring as it spilled from the single spigot and frothed against the basin's blue sides. When had I last taken a bath? And why was I taking one now? On the way out of the salon I had purchased a big green bar of goat's milk soap and bath beads of every color. Now I poured the beads in and watched as they melted, giving the water a glisten it didn't ordinarily have. Careful not to wet my new do, I leaned back and planted one foot firmly on the tub's tiled wall so that my leg was out of the water, a dripping limb oiled and slick. Using my husband's razor, I, for the first time in years, shaved my legs, discovering, as I did that, despite my weight, I still had the curve of a calf, the soft silk of an inner thigh. I shaved my second leg and discovered these facts times two. I stayed in that tub a long, long time. Then I carefully toweled off and put on a dress. I felt, well, lovely. The material swept over the bared landscape of my legs, so smooth to the touch. And where was my depression now?

I walked downstairs to greet my husband, who would be home soon. The kids were on their iPads. "Hi, kids," I said and paused in the entryway to the family room, waiting for them to take notice. The iPads clanged and clicked, the kids' little fingers racing over the screens. "Hi, kids," I said again, and they said, "Hi," without once looking up. I felt let down. I went into the kitchen, barefoot. My husband came through the door. "What happened to you?" he said, dropping his briefcase onto the floor. I cocked my head coquettishly and looked at him. I hadn't said a word to him about Sally or my experiment. I felt emboldened by his surprise. I liked the way his eyebrows arched up and his eyes went wide. I walked over to him and, using my index finger, tilted his chin downward so his lips met mine. I gave him a kiss, a good kiss, a real kiss, the kind of kiss that a woman with a head full of curls could give. He responded in kind. This kiss went on for maybe a minute. I felt infused. I felt as if we were exchanging vitalities. When it was over we smiled at each other in the secret way that couples do when sex is sure to follow. "I got my hair cut," I said. "Did you ever," he replied, and then he said, simply, "Wow."

Sally, it turned out, was a find and worth every penny of the modest two hundred dollars I paid her, sum total, once the experiment was over, which it was not just yet. The next week, Sally took me to Macy's, and I got my face done up at the Clinique counter, where I sat on a high stool and let the lab-coated ladies dab and dress my face, agreeing to buy every product they tried on me. I left with cute little bags filled with still sweeter samples, as well as a big bottle of "Dramatically Different Moisturizing Lotion" and a serum for the bluish area under my eyes. I got a plum lip liner that, when I used it, announced my mouth, plus a matching lipstick that filled in the announcement and gave it some substance. I liked most of all my nut-brown eyeliner and the silver and almond eye shadow, all three colors working in concert to give me a deeper, dreamier look than I had had before. When we were through, Sally took me to the clothing section, where without any further ado she picked up a black jacket with large silver grommets, throwing it over my shoulders as if it were a cape and saying, "Oh, so you." By the time we left Macy's I had several "so you" purchases, a long swirling gray skirt, a peasant blouse with a ruffled neckline, espadrille shoes with straw wedge heels and ribbons that crisscrossed the legs. I had my new makeup and my still springy, sprightly haircut, and the season was changing, the damp, early darkness of winter giving way to a surprisingly warm spring, the rhododendrons blooming early, bursting from their wrapped casings in effusions of purple and red. I intended to wear my new makeup every day, along with the clothes, nice clothes, all of them.

At first it felt funny, no, it felt *hard*, to get up each morning and dress up, applying my makeup carefully, leaning in to the mirror to line my eyes and with the miniature pad sweep silver across my lids, taking the tweezers and plucking my brows into slim little arcs. While some women, maybe many women, find it fun to get dressed up, I did not enjoy the process, my head heavy with stone and sleep. It took discipline to do this, like jogging or taking an aerobics class, forcing myself to flick through the new outfits I'd bought and pick one out for the day, doing this even while my insides were dreary and dark. Dressed, I'd make my way downstairs and pour myself a glass of juice.

After several days of dolling up, I began to notice something strange. After pouring the juice, the pulpless kind, the juice started to shift, the orange intensifying until it seemed to glow in the glass, until it seemed it had been squeezed not from fruit but from gems, the liquid vivid and ice cold even as it flamed at my lips and went down clean and pure. Through the wall-sized windows in my kitchen I started to notice my reflection, my lines leaner and flowing, the skirt so long it puddled at my ankles and swished when I walked, down the hall, into my study. I set the glass of glowing juice on my desk and pulled out my chair to start work. It felt odd to be so dressed because, as a writer, I had no power lunches or afternoon meetings or presentations to attend; it was just me and my word processor. And yet, as the week passed and I put on outfit after outfit, showering, crimping my curly hair, brushing shell-pink rouge across my cheekbones, well, my work started to change. Prior to dressing up I had been a plodding sort of writer, but words were coming to me more quickly now, and characters too, people rising up out of the page and populating my stories with their unique comments and absolutely authentic idiosyncrasies, these fictional characters often accompanied by characters from my past, they too coming back, coming up out of the blank page to meet me because, I could only think, I was finally dressed for the occasion.

In one week's time I wrote two short stories and two essays, and I began to realize that if you want your characters to come to you, you have to be appealing. I was giddy. I grew giddy from the fruits of my labor. In the evenings, in the bathtub, my skin slippery from soap, I could feel what hovered just beneath my surface—my tibia, my deltoids, the bands of muscles and intricate bundles of fibers, the rack of my ribs and the tendons taut in my neck, my surface suggesting to me the suppleness and strength of everything it sheathed. I looked up "skin" in the encyclopedia and confirmed that, sure enough, it is the human body's largest organ, a fact that suggests our surfaces are critical to who we are, not just as the gateway to physical or spiritual depths but a profoundly important web of cells that, in protecting us, gives us form and function. When you touch your surface, you alter the entire hormonal environment of the body beneath, touch signaling certain cells to release a hormone called oxytocin, which stimulates feelings of happiness, connection, love, my clothes caressing my body and beating back depression while I drank down the juice of gems.

Why is it, I wonder, that we live in a culture that so decries the surface on the one hand while emphasizing it on the other, but in both cases misses the essential point? We are told to avoid superficiality even as our culture surrounds us with trinkets and furs, those long coats literally the skinned-off surface of an animal that shares much of our DNA. After two weeks of dressing up and caring for my hair, styling it by crimping the wet curls in my hands after showers, I discovered that what you wear, how you appear when you go to greet the world, is steeply significant not only because the world responds to how you look but, more importantly, because you yourself are altered by whatever mask you make. Wear a tired frumpy face and chances are pretty good that the world will give you its tired frumpy goods, its gray silt and stones, its slow goings and drained days. On the other hand, dress up for the day, insisting on optimism by choosing an outfit that reflects your good taste and, more importantly, your *care*, and you'll find that you have more love in you than you knew. My long-lost libido returned, not the full force of what it once was when I was in my twenties; it was more tempered, somewhat hesitant and shy, my husband having now to fumble with the many buttons and zippers and snaps of my new suits, these barriers to bare skin increasing our arousal and pointing to the purpose, at least in part, of self-adornment.

For the first time in a long time I began to believe in beauty. Not since I was a young teenager had I taken such care in how I looked. I was not able to completely dress my depression away, but when it—Slam! Bam!—reliably returned each morning, it had to tussle with a woman whose heels hoisted her high, who could confidently kneel and cup the faces of her children in her well-tended hands, who knew how to tend to others because she tended to herself, washing my daughter's bleeding knee with the same cloth I swept each morning across my own dream-creased face, erasing the nightmares of seals and sharks, the cloth now blotting up her blood, kissing the wound and leaving on it an impression of my lipsticked mouth, a mark, a stamp, *proof*, that not only was I here but that I could also care.

What I don't know yet is whether I'll hold fast to what I've learned and continue the discipline of daily care that has, without doubt, given me some great good gifts. Why ever would I not, one might wonder, considering my bountiful yield, bedded by my husband, closer to my kids, words coming fast from the tips of my typing fingers. Right now, when I look out my study window, I see a tiny rabbit, a baby no doubt, his fur the color of pearl, his ears pressed flat back against his skull, like small petals that flutter ever so slightly in the spring wind. Are we, I wonder, the only animals who adorn themselves, and if this is so what does that tell us about who we are as humans? There are something like one hundred forty-three types of large land mammals that populate our blue ball, and none of them, excepting ourselves, decorates their bodies, sheathing them in textiles while designing their faces in a range of reds and pinks, blues and browns. That we are the only animal that "dresses up" might suggest that the action lies outside of nature and is therefore somehow twisted, but I doubt this is true. Forty thousand years ago we began to paint on the walls of caves, and shortly after that our earliest human ancestors learned to color their faces with bled berries they found in forests and mashed to pulp in pails. Yes, long before Clairol or Revlon or Clinique stepped onto the scene, the human animal had been driven to decorate his surface, her surface, knowing, intuitively, that our connections to others depend in part on how we look and still more importantly that the sheath we wear suggests the soul beneath.

It's too soon to know whether my newfound belief in the power of beauty will result in a daily discipline, a habit. But I can say, for sure, that entering into beauty did not in any way diminish me as a woman, an artist, a mother, a wife. I have been enhanced, the boil on my back long since healed, nothing there but a small, crescent-shaped scar, the outlines of which I can trace with my fingers, some sort of reminder, a stamp set in my skin. Meanwhile, I look more people in the eye. I bathe my body and the bodies of my children. I dream at night that I have grown twelve feet and am as tall as the trees in the nighttime forest I walk through, tall enough to reach through the bushels of branches and find the small bright birds nestled within, creatures I cup and say *sing to me*. A few days ago a friend suggested we go hiking up Mount Caesar, a relatively small mountain in New Hampshire, not far from where I live. Previously I would have turned down such an invitation, worried that depression would drag down each step, making my ascent too hard, but before I could even consider that as a possibility I found myself saying yes. *Yes*.

And so we went, on a Wednesday, smack-dab in the middle of the week, the trail empty of everyone, the summit sky high, huffing and puffing, my pretty clothes far away in my cedar closet, and I, back, for now, in a pair of ratty shorts and treaded sneakers, my curls plastered flat by sweat. But it didn't matter. In my mind's eye I was the woman with a head full of swirls, a woman whose heels clicked smartly on the stone floor she crossed, a woman in a peasant top typing words that spilled from fingertips groomed for success, and thus we made it. To the top. Huffing and puffing and streaming with sweat we made it. The wind blew around. There was an old large rusty trashcan and a peeling picnic table and the ground gone gold with pine needles. There was a rocky escarpment we crawled out on and looked down into a lake so pure and blue it seemed to possess some sort of living intelligence, a huge eye of water beaming back at us. "Swim?" my friend said. It was unseasonably warm for early April, the temperature well into the eighties. My friend, who is thin, stripped herself of her clothes and then, suddenly, even though I am fat, I followed suit, because I had some chutzpah now. That's what it came down to. Chutzpah. Dressing up gave me the confidence to dress down, to strip. My friend dove first and I dove second, feeling my body arc out over the escarpment and sluice through the summery air and enter the water as fast and fierce as a spear driven downward, everything gone green and then finning fast upward and breaking the surface with a gasp and a shout: "Oh my god!" We laughed and laughed. And then we treaded water silently and swam around. I could see the top of the mountain from where I was and also a field of wildflowers, lupines in every imaginable color and great white wheels of daisies amidst emerald spikes of grass, and it occurred to me then that beauty is not outside of nature; it *is* nature, the natural state of affairs, the way the world is meant to be, and, as for me, because I'm in the world, well, then me too.

As the sun started to set we climbed onto the shore and clambered back up the rocks, our clothes in sun-warmed heaps. We sheathed ourselves and started back down the trail, towards my friend's car, parked in the lot. Even though we were sopping wet, we didn't shiver, our shirts and shorts still soaked in sunlight, the chocolate bar I'd stored in one of my pockets completely melted now so when I thrust my hand in, searching for the necklace I'd removed before I dove, I felt a thick, warm gush and, laughing, I lifted my smeared fingers and licked, and licked, savoring the flavor, grateful I could taste this good.

18

The Mud Is in My Mouth

At some point in my forties, maybe not for the first time and certainly not for the last as that has yet to come, I was walking down a street and saw him, Bad Luck, that is, sitting on his stallion, this in a time of great and personal abundance, or what some might call good luck, writing awards, offers to lecture in Australia, fellowships, and even a lucky lottery ticket for one hundred fifty bucks, scratching away the gold and finding beneath my prize in bold black letters.

And then, in the midst of my abundance, walking down some street on a day like any other, Bad Luck suddenly appeared. Thinking he was handsome or rich or simply amusing, I stupidly agreed to share his saddle, not imagining for even one second the high price I would pay, the prisoner I'd become. Here's what happened: Since that day, since that decision, Bad Luck and I, we've been going at quite a clip, and I can't for the life of me get off while galloping. Bad Luck has a black cowboy hat and a five o'clock shadow you can't help but try to touch, the stubble pricking your finger, that bead of blood always a shock, no matter how often it happens. Am I responsible for Bad Luck, or is he responsible for me? Have we married? Can we divorce? It's hard to think, what with the sound of these hooves in my head. *Ouch.* Have you seen me? Look up. That's not a cloud or a bird or a plane. It's me. Hanging on hard.

Good Luck, they say, likes to visit in threes, or derivatives thereof. I'd say this is true. The discovery of my sanity round about the age of thirty set in motion triptych after triptych of success. Previously a mental patient in a johnny, I became, in a matter of a few years, a productive author, a professor, married, a mother. Money came clattering down, as if I'd stumbled across some rigged slot machine in the sky. These were my years of butter, babies, and books. All my gardens grew. I tried to ignore the fact that Good Luck's gifts likely came with some serious strings attached.

I won an NEA grant and a Knight Science Journalism fellowship, the prize money totaling sixty thousand dollars. Were these rewards deserved or merely bestowed? Of one thing I felt sure: *real* luck has to be earned. You can't simply swallow it like your pills. I pictured a massive collapse, the end of my own personal Ponzi scheme. I celebrated my every milestone with one eye on the second hand of the clock. It never ceased. Time kept moving in joyful circles, like a dog too dumb to know that death is always near.

Despite my great good luck I had many nagging questions, and these many nagging questions about what I deserved led me to actions that some might call "pushing my luck," actions that, I guess, made me the cause rather than the victim of a crash. Pre-Prozac, I dreamt of being a writer and worked hard at a craft I could never claim to have mastered with any confidence, despite my efforts. Post-Prozac, my literary posture improved. Slumped words found their backbones, stood straight, and took to tap dancing. My stories stumbled upon voice, pacing, rhythm, and thus stopped stumbling. I discovered in myself a willingness to be honest. I flaunted that honesty, my raw body, the raw form of my work, and while this was partly in response to my writer's mandate, it was, in equal or unequal parts, a way of testing the limits, only so I could know them, only so I could avoid—or *choose*—a free fall over that sky-high cliff, thereby bringing my stellar career to an abrupt and nearly coveted close, for I did not deserve these prizes and publications and offers of Australia, and worse, it was corrupting me, the urge to write now all mixed up with the urge to win. I was lost, and found, and lost. I was like a blind man, cane tapping his tentative path, or a geologist, eyes closed, running hands over rock, palms sensing the scripted fault lines: *Delve here. No, there.*

As an artistic strategy, my pushing the limits of raw, unfiltered honesty failed. It never got me where I needed to go. It earned me a reputation, I suppose, as a *controversial writer.* It earned me faithful fans in equal proportion to determined detractors. But it did not, this pushing, describe or delineate the edges of my professional bounty so that I might better come to control it. Thus I wrote still harder, faster, riskier, only to find my confusion increasing in proportion to the amount of attention I received, and the more attention I received and the more money I made, the more sure I was that Good Luck would be leaving me soon, and how much the better if I left her before she left me.

No, I don't know his horse's name. Or what sort of underwear he wears. All I can say for sure is that he claimed me like a cowboy, with a whoop and a holler as he lashed out his lasso and snagged my ankle, bringing me down into the dust, me yowling like a calf, and then a cow, and then a woman who has dropped her dignity down the disposal and cannot get it in her grip.

Let's just say, for the sake of story, that the first appearance came three years ago, when Bad Luck was delivered through the mail slot carved in the wooden hunk of our heavy antique door. I distinctly remember this event, how the man-myth and his horse came flying through the letter slot, miniaturized and disguised as lawsuit numero uno.

As with much—but not all—of what followed, I did not do anything, or much (and "Ay, there's the rub," as Hamlet said, feeling for his responsibility), to justify this first lawsuit. And yet, I would also say I did not do much—if anything—to justify the second lawsuit. And then again, I would also say I did not do much—

if anything—to justify the third lawsuit. You see how this sounds? Suspicious, eh? When enough Lemony Snicket sorts of events start to pile up at one's purportedly innocent feet, one would be a fool not to wonder if, or rather *where* (and then again *if*), personal agency enters the picture. Thus we come to the core of my question: Precisely how am I haunted? Back and forth I go, ping-pong turned existential and absurd. *I did it. It did it. I did it. It did it.* To rephrase the question: To what degree, if at all, am I the reason for both my comedy and my tragedy, my riches and my rags?

First, the first lawsuit, which caused the deeply dented coffers. Then, my best friend one day and entirely out of the blue stopped speaking to me, writing in an e-mail, "Stay away from me and I will stay away from you." As if I were diseased, and, who knew, perhaps I was. I began to feel tilted, unwell. I had a huge fight with my literary agent of twenty productive years and left her, or she left me; it matters not. The point: a great gulf came. My favorite aunt, my mother's middle sister, as sweet as my mother was not, died in an automobile accident, driving down the highway without her seatbelt, hitting the car in front, my aunt flying through the windshield, an angel going through glass. My luck turned, and I began my mourning. After my aunt died, our hot-water heater burst and flooded out the basement, destroying all my notebooks, all my earliest attempts at writing, the tiny diary I kept at the age of six, with its little gold lock and minuscule key, warped beyond recognition, this one of my last links to my old home, the one I'd left for a foster family, never to return, left just like Good Luck left me and Bad Luck appeared, pronto, in her place.

And then I was sued a second time, for something equally as ridiculous as the first lawsuit, but the thing about lawsuits is this: you can't just walk away. You have to play the game, get a lawyer; the whole shebang cost me over one hundred thousand dollars, so we went from being well-off to being unwell and also off, but off of what? Off a ledge, an edge, a place of quiet comfort.

And then one day, soon after the second lawsuit had begun, our lawn got a weird disease and then died, and from the dead thatches of sod grew odd purplish plants I'd never seen before. They all had stout scaly stems and broad waxy leaves, and they stormed the yard, multiplying like the rabbits they most certainly were not, daily gaining ground and girth.

Soon after the odd botanical appearance, we began to find small mammals in the once-was grass, their corpses already stiffened, their bodies curled in the corners or simply splayed straight out, flies feasting. At first, we had no idea what might cause such a spree of death nor did I fully comprehend that Good Luck had left for good, so I was slow to take things seriously. My husband and I tried not to giggle through the hedgehog funeral, presided over by the high priest of my daughter and her servant, my four-year-old son, who solemnly covered the cardboard box and placed it in the grave my husband had dug, clearing a patch of the odd plant with a sharp spade.

The morning after the funeral I went outside and tugged on one plant, surprised at how freely its forked roots gave up the ground, dangling their long slippery strings. "Deadly nightshade," the man at the garden center claimed, looking at the limp victim I held out between thumb and forefinger. He snapped on a latex glove and gingerly took the weed from me. *A latex glove?* "It's everywhere in our yard," I said, and I felt something soft in my throat, something, well, gushy.

"I've heard of occasional infestations before," he said. "It's a bitch to get rid of, and you gotta be careful." He placed the plant's corpse on the counter. "This plant," he said, "this plant is one of the most deadly weeds on the East Coast. One bite of its berries and a child's heart stops in a second. I'd keep my kids out of the yard."

Berries?

In August, he told me. The plant becomes a twining vine that unpacks its petals, a fragile purple flower, the seed head stocked with millions of its descendants all dueling to duplicate. At some point mid-month the seed head bursts into birth, the flower furls and falls, and in its place, at summer's end, grow clusters of berries. The horticulturist showed me a botanical drawing of our opponent. In the drawing the flower was long gone, the berries painted a rich red, dangling on the slender stem like a lumpy scarlet scrotum. According to the horticulturist, the berries are surprisingly sweet to the taste, attractive to all manner of life forms who know no better: raccoons, skunks, hedgehogs, minors.

It was well into summer, then, and my corner of the globe was wilted in warmth. The sidewalks sizzled. The flowers along the fences had long since fainted, their faces hanging sideways. Only the nightshade thronged. We had resigned ourselves to the necessity of chemical intervention lest the hedgehog lead to a swan lead to a prince or princess.

I spent a few hundred bucks on contractor-grade herbicide, thigh-high rubber boots, huge plastic goggles, pale-blue gloves. Sweating from every gland, I tromped around our yard, pumping the valve, poison arcing from the plastic spout and splashing with a small sound onto the thriving green leaves. The next morning, the nightshade looked, well, unsettled, as though, perhaps, every stalk was being sued. By evening, the purple flowers had rolled up and dropped off. Within a week, the stalks were dead and brown, their previously plump vines stringy, the plants arced and twisted in what seemed expressions of agony. Our yard still looked infested, but not with nightshade anymore. It looked infested with death. And not a single scream.

I can't possibly tell all the terrible things that happened to me. By now I'd been through two of the three lawsuits that came my way, an infestation, the toaster caught on fire. We went in search of sunshine, to Florida, and all our luggage got lost and was never found, so to this day our brown bags are somewhere circling and circling the globe. I started fighting with my spouse; this was—what— 2006? And then 2007 came in a gust of mild garbagey-smelling January wind, the winter melt laced with brown, sloppy dog turds on every city sidewalk. The paths around our more rural home smelled as though they'd been made from septic sludge. I felt my words wobble when I wrote. Periods turned into question marks, which marched off the page and stood sentry in my head. *Was this word right was that word right was this word right?* It finally became clear to me that, at some point I could not quite determine, Good Luck had definitely—and with finality—departed, on to bigger and better pastures. Previously a veritable font of authorial productivity, I felt my spouts close. The blank page is, in fact, far from blank. Stare long enough into its creamy smother and you feel yourself start to gasp.

Less, I'm sure, is more in situations of negative abundance. Thus I'll try to do this quickly. Our house began to rot. Or maybe it was always rotting, and I began to realize it. During an unseasonal rainstorm, a chunk of our foundation came loose, and when the wet weather passed we found the chunk on our neighbor's lawn. Slates slid from our previously sturdy roof. Water dribbled down our walls, the color of rust sometimes, and then sometimes the color of soot. I'd always loved our house; we'd been living in it, a small saltbox with a single stained-glass window in its narrow hall, for over three years now, a house set on acres and acres of pasture and forest, the trees so tall and old a man's huge arms could not circle their massive majestic trunks.

Good Luck and Bad Luck have similar plot lines. They start slowly, gather motion, roll, then rise to a crescendo, and, following the basic laws of physics (Remember this from seventh grade? *An object in motion remains in motion unless . . .*), stop only when acted upon by an outside force.

Thus my panic, for what would the outside force be if not Bad Luck's sole equal and opposite—Good Luck—with her honey hair and high heels, long gone from me now, involved with her new clients.

Humanoids emerged on this earth two million years ago, and since that time there have been on the order of a quarter-million regal philosophers who thought through issues as diverse as time and grief, evil and isolation, the blessed and the cursed, the whys and wherefores. The great playwright Sophocles dandled luck in his lap and wove it into every act, and still, in the end, he could not name its ingredients or its origins. If the most noble philosophers pondering the issue for, say, the last twelve thousand years have not been able to unpack luck, why on earth, so long as I'm on Earth, would I? Sometimes giving up is a form of grace.

My cognitive revolution occurred in—so appropriate—the sweet rainy spring of 2009, when the clouds emptied themselves of their water weight and emerged, come June, as lean, clean lines of white and the palest of pinks. The rain-drenched earth yielded up its goods in excess, so ripe strawberries, as nubby as tongues between large green leaves, emerged everywhere in our garden, the weeds washed away, the loam beneath as black as melted chocolate, the fiery-yellow flowers standing in stark and gorgeous contrast to the ground. In June, the flowers bobbed and nodded when the breeze blew, as if agreeing with me. Yes. Call it quits. Enough wondering why. Or when. Or if. Enough examination.

And yet, what does one *do* after quitting? I'd been struggling for so long, puzzle piecing for so long, meditating for so long on my fortune and its reversal, trying for so long to woo my ex–best friend back to me and to repair what was beyond repair with my literary agent, working and working, chewing and chewing: how to give all that up and simply sit? I have never liked meditation. The mandate to breathe always makes me feel like I am choking. The practices of Buddhism are not my strong suit.

"Let's build a pond," I said to my husband that summer, and he, perhaps sensing that I needed a project other than myself, agreed, and so we took up our shovels, together for the first time in a long time. In the abandoned, weed-eaten field behind our rural home, a field the prior owner scraped of its top soil to sell for a fat fee, we excavated the hard earth, hurling sharp spades into its stone-studded skin, splitting it sideways, subsoil yielding up the glossiest, wriggliest worms, and those stones, everywhere, flat and round, veined and mottled, but all, every one, mysteriously smooth, as if they'd been pounded for millennia by the sea. "Perhaps they have," my husband said, holding in his palm a gorgeous purple globe, a red arterial scrawl just visible beneath its opaque, violet skin. "After all, this was once the ocean," he said, gesturing with his hand to the land all around us, the tall grass in the healthy far fields rippling like the hide of some huge beast; picture that. We were once covered. It comforted me, for a reason I can't say. You find your blankets; ultimately, you do. I pulled the sea around me, a salty shawl.

And, comforted but still uncomfortable, I, and we, continued to dig. The sun swelled hotter, higher, as the days went by, and on the solstice our sun was pierced on its pointed peak, spinning and spinning madly, this fire-star, our *raison d'etre*. They say to never stare into the sun, but I did. I stared straight into its blackened stove-belly and saw for minutes afterwards dark shapes dance before my eyes. I posed no questions. I got no answers.

Meanwhile, we dug ourselves in and, paradoxically, out to a depth of five feet, ice-cold lemonade cracking the thick glassine thirst that coated our throats, proving relief was possible.

"I want ten feet," my husband said, eyeing the modest hole. "If we're going to make a pond, I want it deep enough so I can do cannonballs without worrying about my ass."

This seemed reasonable to me, so we hired a yellow machine with a steel claw, and the machine gnawed out another five feet, so at the end we had a crater that descended deep into the earth, the tapered sides taupe colored, at night the hole so impenetrably dark, so utterly mysterious one could almost imagine the tiny flickering lights of China deep in the deepest distance, a world beyond our world.

Ponds, like breasts, are not meant to be made. They are meant to simply occur. When one makes a thing like a pond or for that matter a breast, one must resort, unless incredibly lucky, to unnatural interventions; in the case of breast-making, saline implants or chunks of fine flesh culled from a chunky bottom; in the case of ponds, plastic liners or concrete, some way to hold the water. We'd resigned ourselves to a liner, all twenty-five hundred pounds of Firestone nontoxic rubber.

It was July then, and the rains resumed, and our pond-making stalled while we were pelted. The rain came down like a temper, a tantrum, beating its billions of fists against the hoods of cars, the roofs of houses. Tears of rain snaked their way beneath the loosened slates, slid down the walls, so the walls wept while I watched; I practiced watching. *How do walls weep? Why do walls weep? Can walls weep? Do weeping walls stop weeping?* I might have had such crazy questions if I had succumbed to my mind's inclinations; but I did not succumb. I watched the rain. I waited it out, and, in the waiting, my body began to rain right along with the world. I rained droplets, sweated drops, the humidity coating me, its hand across my mouth.

I detest clichés, but then again, there's a reason why certain phrases have attained immortality as clichés. I cannot think of a better way of saying that when you let something go, it frequently comes back to you. I let go of the search for understanding my bad luck, and in doing that, I also let go of the hope embedded in that search: that, by understanding, I might come to control my fortune, which I would swiftly reverse once I figured out the stick shift. I let the wheel go, watched Good Luck and Bad Luck disappear into their separate mists, lost sight of them completely in the rain, and then the rain stopped. The clouds cleared. They cleared swiftly, dramatically, like a stage set or a movie; we went from black to stunning blue, the day emerging at once wet and crisp, the trees dripping jewels, the flowers drunk on drinking, their heads lolling with dizzy delight, rivulets etched into our earth, showing us which way the rain ran, downhill, of course, heading, all water, straight for our yet-to-be-pond. We had ordered the liner, and right this minute it was en route, rolled like a massive scroll, a Torah made of rubber, on some truck, halfway between Minnesota and Massachusetts. Understand, the liner was key and, therefore, even though it ensured a synthetic wetland, we couldn't wait to receive it. Our pond depended upon it. The liner would at once contain and seal the pond, allowing it to exist while ensuring its fraudulent nature. Unnaturally sealed up, our pond would require expensive aeration systems and flashy pumps that would circulate the water 24/7, sending a no-no message to mosquitoes seeking stagnant fluids in which to hatch their larvae.

And now, after rain, with only a few days left *before* the shipment was to arrive, we followed the water's path to our half-made pond. We weren't going to see if it held water; we assumed it would not. We were going to see if the pounding rainfall had destroyed the plant shelves we had so carefully sculpted.

I think we heard it before we saw it, the sound of *plop plop plop*. Ben says he heard gurgling, not plopping, but I don't see how that's possible. I heard plopping, and then, peering over the sculpted lip of our hole, I saw emerald frogs arcing from bank to bank, missing by long shots, falling into what could be called a massive puddle or could be called a . . . a . . . *pond*, for the hole was holding water, against all odds, against all rules, because dirt in New England does not hold water, but, well, this dirt did. "Clay," an aquascape contractor, told us a few days later, when he came out to see our little miracle, our piece of great good luck, the liner shipment cancelled, $12K returned to our account. "You've got clay here it seems," the pond professional said, grabbing a chunk of the saturated stuff and letting it ooze through his fist. "You know," he said, "you're really, really lucky. You won't need a liner. Pond people would kill to have your soil."

I started to laugh then, because I knew no one would kill to have my soil. Of this I was positive.

Still, there are times when clocks stop and awareness of the terrible temporary nature of your world gets suspended in some liminal, summer-like state, so your life hangs like a long afternoon in a perfect mid-July, the roses rose-red, their mouths yawning wide as if in perpetual surprise, or sleepiness. And that was what our sudden luck was like. We didn't ponder its temporary nature; we just enjoyed it. The kids whooped with delight, stripped off their clothes, and went racing down the embankment, skidding, stumbling, finally belly flopping into the half-filled crater, muddy and foggy but delightfully cool and totally ours. All day the kids played in the pond we'd made, caught frogs, pried stones from the field and let them cannonball down deep into the deepest part. The children emerged from the murky water at sunset, sun-baked and flaking mud; we hosed them down outside, brown giving way to a deeper brown, the bodies of my estivating progeny.

I woke early the next morning to a sound. A step. Something emerging from the forest that lined our land. I don't know how I could have heard her, for she was too far away, but I swear I heard her step, her delicate cloven foot landing lightly on the still soaking leaves, coming closer, closer, while I slipped out of bed to watch at the window. The doe seemed to be of suede, with a fine shapely head and ears at once triangular and furred. Her long neck arced out, lowered her head like a lever, and I saw her drink the accumulated rain our whole pond held, for her, and us.

I believed something was over, had passed then. I felt I had climbed to the top of a steep spiral staircase and now I stood looking down at the vortex of steel from the final landing.

That afternoon, Benjamin took the kids for ice cream, and I planned to try the pond out for myself.

Where we live: on thirty-eight acres forty-eight miles from Boston, MA, but forty-eight worlds apart. Our town is tiny, rural, the streets astir with horses and cars in equal number. At rush hour, carts roll down the road, pulled by geldings with black blinders siding their angular faces, and every morning the sun rises from behind the mountain, first its rays snaking upward and then at last the yolk of yellow yanked suddenly into the sky, as if pulled on a chain, or some string, held in the hand of god. And every night that same sun sets in reverse order, first the yolk, aflame now, streaming salmon pinks and hemorrhage-red from its bruised body, that yolk drops down abruptly behind the stony ridge, leaving its rays to linger aimlessly, until, one by one, they fizzle out almost audibly, and the darkness is a-chirp with crickets and other creatures.

Where we live, a neighbor can be eight acres away.

I walk around naked where we live. When it's warm, I do this, despite my weight, because of my weight, I do this and revel in my privilege.

Thus, I stripped to my skin and, without even the screen of sun lotion, walked down the dirt path to the pond, which looked so peaceful, like a huge cup of tea on an earthen saucer. Dragonflies glinted above it, snacking on mosquitoes, and way down at the bottom, frogs skimmed the water, their back legs flung behind their goopy bodies, clowns, every one.

Now I made my way down the embankment we had made, surprised at how steep it actually was. We had tried to dig the sides to no more than a slope of twenty degrees, but this could not have been twenty degrees. Gravity put both his hands on my back and pushed me, so my cautious walk turned into a stumble, and then a slip, and then before I could say *catchascatchcan*, I went lickety-split into the pond, sliding to my destination on my bare ass, cool clay caking my palms and parts.

And then I was in, swimming around, pedaling in the water, flinging my legs like the frogs, breast stroking back and forth with them. Delightful. Five days of heavy rains had not managed to fill 'er up to ten feet. I'd say our pond was filled to four feet ten inches, maximum. I know this because when I finally stood up, I, at five feet, could stand with my head above water, stand, that is, in the center, the deepest point of the pond, which is where I stood now, with my head above water, and then I walked forward, towards the embankment, our steep-sloped shore, having had my fill, ready to get out, standing for a second in the shallow end to admire what we'd made, the water calm and lapping. I stood, water at my ankles. I stood for no more than maybe five seconds, gathering myself to get out.

And that is when it happened. Not slowly; it happened suddenly, as though a rug had been pulled, because suddenly I was sinking, the muddy bottom collapsing out from under me, my flailing feet searching for water but instead stuck in sucking mud, and I could not stop the sucking. I've never felt anything comparable. I had never known the earth was capable of collapsing in this manner; my standing spot was having a nervous breakdown of some sort, melting down into some substance all ooze and excrement, some voracious devilish substance gobbling me up, or down; down, I went, not even thinking to scream.

I was, then, sunk to my knees, my thighs; it happened fast. I recall feeling in a flash how hot and heavy the afternoon sun was on my head, like a hand, pushing me down, this image in a flash of a flash, and then disappeared, just darkness, and now the mud was at my midpoint. I kept going.

My life did not roll before my eyes.

I did not process my regrets, or my loves, or my luck, for that matter.

I lost all thought; I shed my status as a noun and became pure verb, at one with the plot I was quite literally sucked into. I was going down, and I needed to find a way up, and out; but I was no match for the mud. My muscles were irrelevant in the mud. I could not quite grasp this fact at first, because I have always thought that, if caught in a natural disaster, your muscles would save you or sink you; it was all about strength, was it not? And yet here, no matter how hard I strained and clawed, it made not one whit of difference; I was clawing at mush, at mash; clawing at cloud, pushing against emptiness, each tiny, solid center my feet seemed to find collapsing still further inward.

A long time passed. This I know. So perhaps my struggles *did* do me some good, did slow the sinking; the sun was far westward when the mud crept past my neck and pressed up against my pursed lips, clasping my whole head just below my flaring nostrils. "Where the fuck is my family," I thought, and then, in a flare of rage, "This is one hell of an ice-cream cone they're all eating."

Now, the mud was in my mouth.

Up my nose.

I started choking, spitting, but whenever I spat, the more mud was in my mouth. I could still breathe. I could breathe well enough to weep, and weep I then did, and my tears merged with the mud and made it still muddier. And once again, then, I saw that, quite literally, there was nothing I could do. There was simply no way out. No amount of understanding, or struggle, would crack the code of quicksand, which this essentially was, and I was tired. So very tired.

I tried once more to thrash my way upward, and then exhaustion captured me completely, and I slumped in my mud and tasted its taste: drenched darkness, thick salt, shredded plant. I tasted it all: the earth, the depth, the darkness, the minerals, the fire, the water, the loam the clay the seeds the salt the weeping the wanting the living the dying; I tasted it all because I was forced to. I slumped in my mud and sampled the whole world.

I didn't know that if you are ever caught in quicksand, rule one is *not* to struggle. I stopped struggling because I could not continue.

And once I stopped, the mud stopped with me. In fact, it was as though the entire earth just came to a quiet halt, with me. I hung there, entombed, suspended between here and there, then and now, with nothing sucking; just stopped. Dangling in density, utterly liminal, still weeping.

But even in tears I took note of how stopping had helped. Once I stopped, so too did the sinking. I'd like to know why this is, but I have not had the time to look into it.

And then, after minutes or hours, mosquitoes still nibbling on my scalp, the suspension transformed itself into an ever-so-slight upward lift. I felt it, a tectonic shift, a northward shrug, the earth in all its layers quite literally lifting me out of my mess.

Now I stayed very still, afraid to even wriggle my toes, because clearly there was a connection between the stillness in my body and the upward movement of the world. I was in mud, but miles beneath my feet the tectonic plates held me aloft, ground their gears, and then urged me skyward, so eventually my mouth emerged, my neck, my shoulders, my breasts, black moguls, my belly, black balloon; I rose in increments standing still, doing nothing. I rose, or, rather, the earth rose me, rewarded me, and once my stomach was out, I flung my whole self forward, clung to the embankment, hauled myself high and higher still, the pond's lip just inches away now. And only then did I allow myself these images: phoenix, swan, mermaid, rising from her own excessive froth, finding her land legs, ecstatic not because of talent, and surely not because of luck (but then again precisely because of luck, her gifts sometimes gaudy, sometimes simple, she favors the prepared, perhaps, but, as far as I'm concerned, everything I get, both good and bad, yes, everything I get starts to go as soon as I feel it on my fingers. . . .).

And yet this I can count on: I made my way up over the embankment and stepped on solid ground. Imagine what I must have looked like from far away, my family far away, pulling in, tumbling out of the Subaru, seeing a black woman with a silver halo of hair stumbling across an infertile field, tears making tracks in her Nigerian face, this is what I must have looked like from the outside. But from the inside? Well, that's a different story.

I was on a whole different pole but not polarized, no, no longer. I was simply on the inside, in a shining bright room, a small bundle of fire flickering in the hearth, well-steeped tea in a saucer by my side, beloved book in my lap. I looked around. Outside butterflies massed by the windows, so many species, so many colors, such a plethora of filmy wings. I could just barely hear them beat, just barely smell the garden pouring its perfume. I was inside, in a space and a grace called *this place here is home*, and I held out my hands and my children came running and my husband came walking and the butterflies came flying and the frogs came hopping and the locusts came shrieking and Job came limping and god came on his chariot and Bad Luck on his stallion and Good Luck in her Mercedes and my children on their lean and thank-the-lord-healthy legs and my husband powered by his steady and thank-the-lord healthy heart, they all came, such a crowd beyond counting, five football stadiums came as I held out my hands and everyone ran and I let them inside. We went inside and lit a small fire, and I told them this tale, this story, of sinking, of stumbling, of summer, and of finally finding some stillness, small fire, the fall of my footsteps always in my ears here; *fall fall fall*, the sound no longer ominous, oddly sweet now, like the autumn that is coming, like the leaves that will blaze, like the trees turning to torches while I watch all this, my hands held out, in humility, for balance, my borders; *here is where I stand.*

Acknowledgments

These essays were written over a period of so many years that it is impossible to thank all the people who had a hand in helping me, in ways small and large. My husband, Benjamin Alexander, has been perhaps the one constant, continual presence during the time span these essays describe; he has read every one, at times with a grimace, because he, unlike me, is a deeply private person who cannot fathom the autobiographical impulse, which is not, as people think, a narcissistic need to perform on your own personal stage but rather a reaching out, from some deeply personal space, a reaching out into the world in the hopes of hearing your words echo in the lives of others who, like you, share your struggles and your joys. I'd like to thank, therefore, my readers, many of whom e-mail me to let me know my work has reverberated for them; this is the greatest gift a writer can receive. I'd also like to thank my children; they have enchanted me and enriched me in so many ways, lending me language and image, plot and prism, allowing me time and space to write while also insisting that I return to the real world each afternoon, the world of peanut butter and homework, spelling tests and track meets. My children are both inspirations and anchors, as well as amazing individuals, and becoming more so every day.

After I gathered these essays together, which was in and of itself a significant task as they were strewn across computers and hard drives and disparate publications, I sat down to read them in the order my editor at Beacon Press, Helene Atwan—whom I also need to thank for her masterful mind and vision—had suggested. And I was, well, a little shocked, a little shaken, by what was on the page.

These were indisputably my essays, but some I hadn't seen or touched for ten years or more, and thus reading them in a chronological arrangement was like peering at my past through a hole someone had punched in the air. There I was, pregnant and despairing. Here I was, still bleeding from my mastectomy, my daughter's words and comfort—remember that? I did. I saw myself starkly, a self capable of greediness, small heartedness, fear, and also love. It was uncomfortable to see myself from so many angles, rendered so starkly, all jagged and ripped and incapable, at least at times.

Each essay in this book was written "on assignment" (though here you are seeing the full-length versions, sometimes two and three times longer than what was first published), and thus I always took these essays less seriously than my "real work," my books, which I wrote not for money but for love. And yet, looking at these arranged essays, I realized that, without ever knowing it, or meaning to, I had told a sober, serious, and scathingly honest account of one woman's life straddling two centuries.

I want to thank each and every person who put up with me during those years. I want to thank the friends who nurtured me, despite my prickly nature. I want to thank, especially, the editors at the magazines from which the assignments issued, specifically Laurie Abraham at *Elle*, and Paula Derrow, who was at *Self*, and Deborah Way and Pat Towers at *O, The Oprah Magazine*, and Cathleen Medwick and Nanette Varian at *More*; I want to thank every editor at every women's magazine where these essays all initially appeared.

Women's magazines—they get a bad rap. If you can publish in the *New Yorker* or the *Atlantic*, then you can publish with pride, but to publish in a glossy with advertisements for lingerie and lip gloss and attendant articles about lovemaking techniques—that can be embarrassing. And I *was* always a bit embarrassed about publishing in "women's magazines," as they don't have the pomp and polish, the intellectual heft, of some of their more serious competitors. And yet, I now see that I was wrong to feel that way. *Elle, Self, O, More,* and the other women's magazines that published my autobiographical work were willing to show their readers much more than eyeliner and thongs. My essays are about the darker aspects of being a white, middle-class female in our times. These magazines, for more than a decade, allowed, even encouraged, me to tell the truth about my life, the whole unruly, unpretty truth, which they then published, proving, along the way, that "women's magazines" are capable of carrying complex stories about difficult subjects to their vast audiences.

In making this book, I have revised my notions about women's magazines and want to encourage you to do the same. These glossies have provided me with pages to tell stories that had no gleam or gloss in them, stories my editors celebrated each and every time, their mission, I now see, to bring to their readers honest accounts of what it is like to live inside a mind and body with two x's in every single cell, this body, this mind, grim, difficult, delighted, in every state, in every way, with thanks to all the hands held out, from all these magazines. My stories exist because they do.